# MINI CROSS STITCH
# ORNAMENTS

LEISURE ARTS, INC. • Maumelle, Arkansas

# Danish Angel

| DMC | X | 1/4 | BS | FK |
|---|---|---|---|---|
| white | ▣ | ▢ | | |
| 340 | ▲ | ▲ | | |
| 402 | ◱ | ◦ | | |
| 413 | | | ◢ | |
| 666 | ⊠ | | | ● |
| 701 | ◆ | ◆ | | |
| 701 | | | ◢ | |
| 703 | H | H | | |
| 725 | ★ | | | |
| 775 | ✖ | ✗ | | |

| DMC | X | 1/4 | BS |
|---|---|---|---|
| 815 | ◢ | | |
| 815 | | | ◢ |
| 920 | | | ◢ |
| 947 | ❤ | | |
| 948 | ⊡ | ⊡ | |
| 956 | ◨ | | |
| 957 | Z | Z | |
| 3078 | ◇ | ◇ | |
| 3776 | ◣ | ◤ | |

**32w x 43h** – Design stitched on 14 count white Aida using 3 strands for cross stitch, 1 strand for backstitching, 1 strand for French knots.

◢ Cutting line for Aida

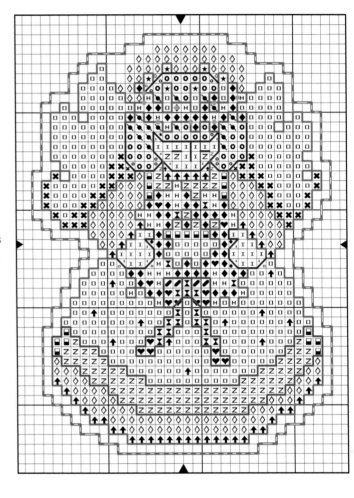

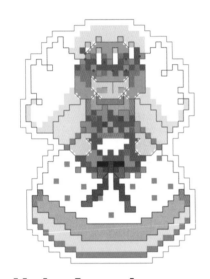

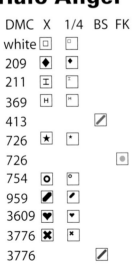

# Halo Angel

| DMC | X | 1/4 | BS | FK |
|---|---|---|---|---|
| white | ▣ | ▢ | | |
| 209 | ◆ | ◆ | | |
| 211 | ⊡ | ⊡ | | |
| 369 | H | H | | |
| 413 | | | ◢ | |
| 726 | ★ | ★ | | |
| 726 | | | | ● |
| 754 | ◔ | ◦ | | |
| 959 | ◢ | ◢ | | |
| 3609 | ❤ | ❤ | | |
| 3776 | ✖ | ✗ | | |
| 3776 | | | ◢ | |

**25w x 33h** – Design stitched on 14 count white Aida using 3 strands for cross stitch, 1 strand for backstitching, 1 strand for French knots.

◢ Cutting line for Aida

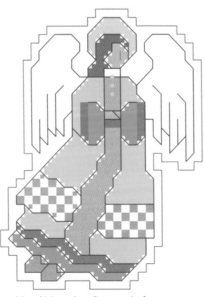

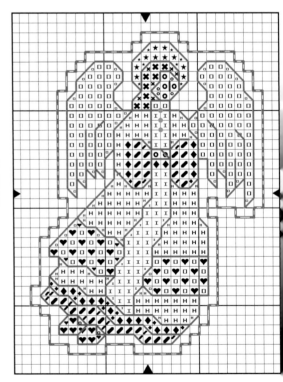

## Bow

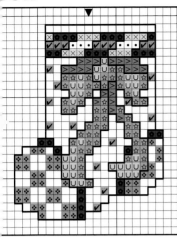

## Patchwork

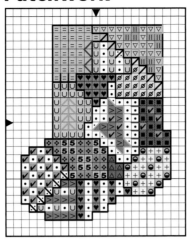

## Cardinal

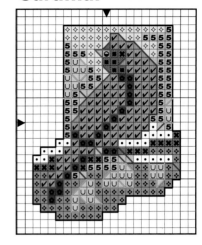

## Moon

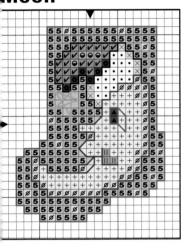

## Nutcracker

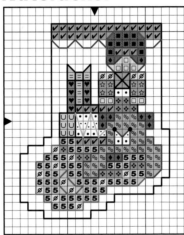

## Quilt Block

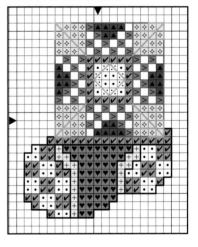

## Singing Angel

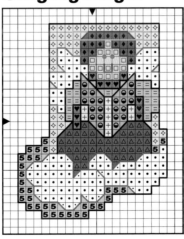

## Lights

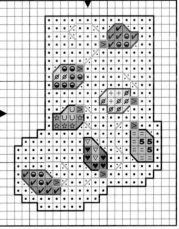

| X | DMC | ¼X | B'ST |
|---|---|---|---|
| • | white | | |
| ▲ | 208 | | |
| ■ | 310 | | ✓ |
| ▲ | 311 | | ✓ |
| ◔ | 402 | | |
| | 413 | | ✓ |
| ✕ | 415 | | |
| ▽ | 605 | | |
| ◒ | 608 | | |
| ✔ | 666 | | ✓ |
| ☆ | 702 | | |
| U | 703 | | |
| + | 743 | | |
| | 775 | | |
| 5 | 813 | | |
| ◉ | 814 | | ✓ * |
| | 825 | | |
| ✖ | 898 | | ✓ * |
| ‖ | 899 | | |
| ▷ | 909 | | ✓ † |
| ◆ | 921 | | |
| ▢ | 945 | | |
| ∅ | 973 | | ✓ ★ |
| ═ | 996 | | |
| ▼ | 3607 | | |
| ● | 310 French knot | | |
| ◉ | 413 French knot | | |

∗ 814 for Cardinal, 898 for Angel, Lights, and Nutcracker

† Use **2** strands for Lights and long stitches in Quilt Block.

★ Use **1** strand and long stitches in Nutcracker. Use **2** strands for Angel and long stitchs in Moon.

**19w x 24h each** – Designs stitched on 14 count white perforated plastic using 3 strands for cross stitch, 1 strand for backstitching except where noted.

# Rocking Bear

| DMC | X | 1/4 | BS | FK |
|-----|---|-----|-----|-----|
| white | ▢ | ▫ | | |
| 310 | ■ | | | |
| 310 | | | ╱ | ● |
| 402 | ✚ | ＋ | | |
| 413 | | | ╱ | |
| 414 | ◢ | ◢ | | |
| 415 | H | H | | |
| 666 | ♥ | ♥ | | |

| DMC | X | 1/4 | BS |
|-----|---|-----|-----|
| 741 | ○ | | |
| 954 | ⊥ | ⊥ | |
| 956 | △ | △ | |
| 957 | I | I | |
| 971 | ✕ | ✕ | |
| 975 | | | ╱ |
| 3776 | ◆ | ◆ | |
| 3856 | L | L | |

**36w x 42h** – Design stitched on 14 count white Aida using 3 strands for cross stitch, 1 strand for backstitching, 1 strand for French knots.

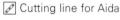 Cutting line for Aida

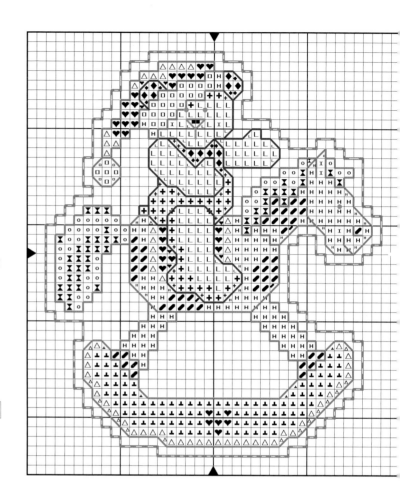

# Jingle Bear

| DMC | X | 1/4 | BS | FK |
|-----|---|-----|-----|-----|
| white | ▢ | ▫ | | |
| 310 | ■ | ■ | | |
| 310 | | | ╱ | ● |
| 402 | ○ | ° | | |
| 413 | | | ╱ | |
| 666 | ♥ | ♥ | | |
| 703 | ◆ | ◆ | | |

| DMC | X | 1/4 | BS |
|-----|---|-----|-----|
| 742 | ★ | ★ | |
| 798 | ✕ | | |
| 809 | ⑤ | | |
| 815 | ✖ | | |
| 956 | Z | z | |
| 3753 | ⊓ | | |
| 3776 | ◢ | ◢ | |

**35w x 42h** – Design stitched on 14 count white Aida using 3 strands for cross stitch, 1 strand for backstitching, 1 strand for French knots.

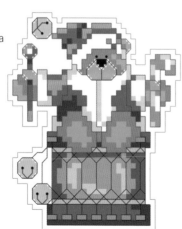 Cutting line for Aida

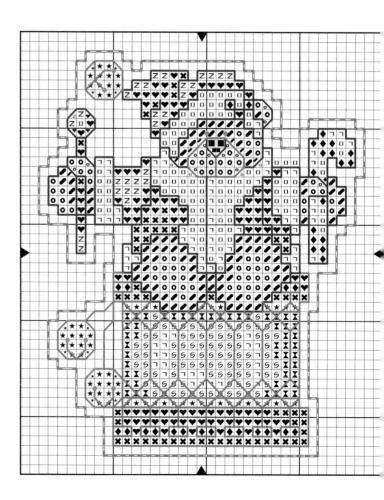

## Kitty

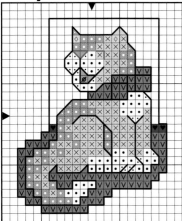

## Snowflakes

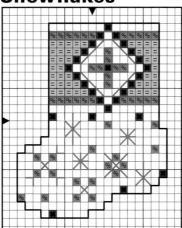

## Santa with Gift

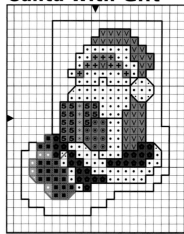

## House

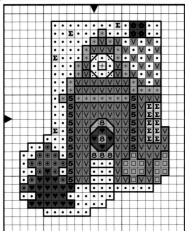

## Waving Santa

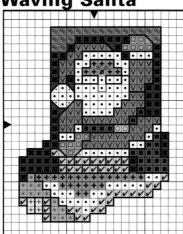

## Cow

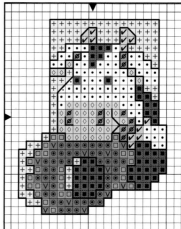

## Painting Elf

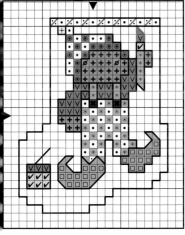

## Meadow Snowman

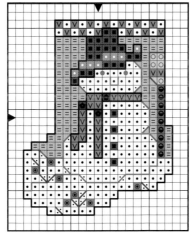

## St. Nick

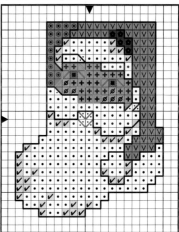

| X | DMC | ¼X | B'ST | | X | DMC | ¼X | B'ST | | X | DMC | ¼X | B'ST |
|---|---|---|---|---|---|---|---|---|---|---|---|---|---|
| • | white | | | | = | 775 | | | | ✳ | 996 | | |
| ■ | 310 | | *  | | % | 813 | | † | | 5 | 3607 | | |
| ◉ | 413 | | | | ◆ | 814 | | | | ◉ | 310 French Knot | | |
| ⊠ | 414 | | | | ✹ | 825 | | * | | ● | 413 French Knot | | |
| ✔ | 415 | | | | ◉ | 898 | | | | | | | |
| ◇ | 605 | | | | ø | 899 | | † | | | | | |
| 8 | 608 | | | | ▼ | 909 | | | | | | | |
| V | 666 | | † | | | 921 | | | | | | | |
| ◉ | 702 | | | | + | 945 | | | | | | | |
| ▢ | 703 | | | | ◯ | 972 | | | | | | | |
| + | 743 | | | | Σ | 973 | | | | | | | |

**19w x 24h each** - Designs were stitched on 14 count white perforated plastic using 3 strands for cross stitch, 1 strand for backstitching, 1 strand for French knots.

* 310 for Kitty, Santa with Gift, Cow, and St Nick. 825 for Snowflakes and Meadow Snowman.

† 666 for Waving Santa, Painting Elf, Meadow Snowman, and St Nick. 813 for Snowflakes. 899 for Kitty.

## Reindeer

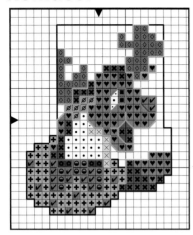

## Candy Cane

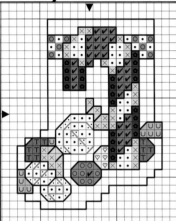

## Sledding Bear

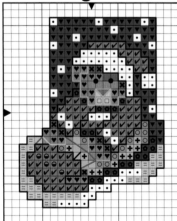

## Sleeping Bear

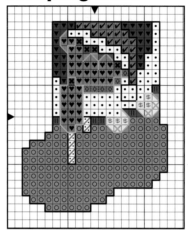

## Santa Bear

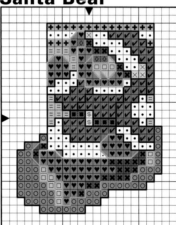

## Goose

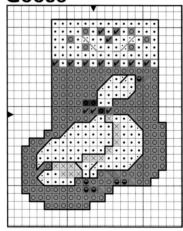

## Joy

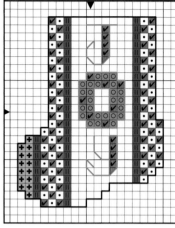

## Poinsettia

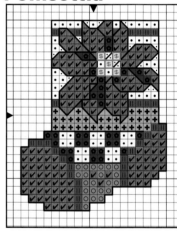

## Boot

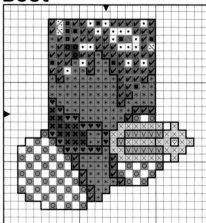

**19w x 24h each, except Boot 23w x 24h -**
Designs stitched on 14 count white perforated plastic using 3 strands for cross stitch, 1 strand for backstitching, 1 strand for French knots except where noted.

| X | DMC | ¼X | B'ST | | X | DMC | ¼X | B'ST |
|---|-----|-----|------|---|---|-----|-----|------|
| · | white | ◹ | | | ◲ | 898 | ◸ | ◹ |
| ■ | 310 | | ◹ * | | ◌ | 899 | ◸ | |
| | 310 | | ◹ † | | ▥ | 909 | ◸ | ◹ * |
| ◤ | 311 | ◸ | | | ✕ | 921 | ◸ | |
| ♥ | 402 | ◸ | | | ▢ | 945 | ◸ | |
| ☑ | 413 | | ◹ | | $ | 972 | ◻ | |
| ✕ | 415 | ◻ | | | U | 996 | ◸ | |
| ◉ | 608 | ◸ | | | T | 3607 | ◸ | |
| ✔ | 666 | ◸ | ◹ ★ | | ● | 898 | **French knot** | |
| ◎ | 702 | ◸ | ◹ * | | | | | |
| ✚ | 703 | ◸ | | | | | | |
| ♡ | 743 | ◻ | | | | | | |
| ▤ | 775 | ◸ | | | | | | |
| ▦ | 813 | | | | | | | |
| ▩ | 814 | ◸ | ◹ ★ | | | | | |

\* 310 for Reindeer and Boot. 702 for Joy and Goose. 909 for Candy Cane.

† Use **2** Strands of floss

★ 666 for Sleeping Bear, Joy, Candy Cane, Poinsettia and Goose. 814 for Reindeer.

# Santa

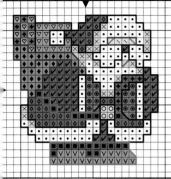

0w x 20h

# Tree

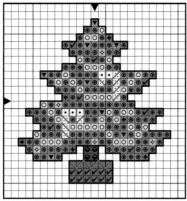

21w x 22h

# Drummer

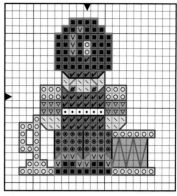

19w x 21h

# Snowman

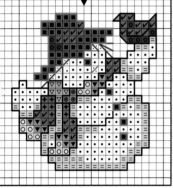

20w x 21h

# Wreath

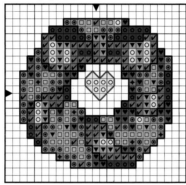

21w x 20h

# Santa Face

21w x 22h

# Gingerbread Man

20w x 21h

# Angel

21w x 21h

# Instruments

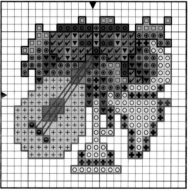

22w x 21h

| X | DMC | ¼X | B'ST |
|---|---|---|---|
| • | white | ◪ | |
| ■ | 310 | ◪ | ◪ * |
| ◨ | 400 | ◪ | ◪ † |
| + | 402 | ◪ | |
| | 413 | | ◪ |
| ▼ | 414 | ◪ | |
| ✕ | 415 | ◻ | |
| ▽ | 518 | | |
| ✔ | 666 | ◪ | ◪ ★ |
| ○ | 676 | ◻ | |
| ▼ | 699 | | ◪ * |
| ◉ | 702 | ◪ | |
| ▢ | 704 | | |
| = | 775 | | |
| ✚ | 783 | | |

| X | DMC | ¼X | B'ST |
|---|---|---|---|
| ◙ | 814 | | ◪ ★ |
| ◇ | 815 | ◪ | |
| ◿ | 899 | | |
| ◺ | 945 | ◻ | |
| ◈ | 964 | | |
| ▼ | 970 | ◪ | |
| ✦ | 3607 | | |
| ♡ | 3609 | | |
| ◆ | 3776 | ◪ | |

*310 for for Santa, Drummer, Snowman, Gingerbread Man, and Angel. 699 for Tree (**2** strands)

†Use long stitches for mandolin strings in Instruments.

★666 for Tree and Gingerbread Man (**1** strand) and Drummer (**2** strands). 814 for Santa and Santa Face.

Designs stitched on 14 count white perforated plastic using 3 strands for cross stitch, 1 strand backstitching except where noted.

13

# Wintergreen Candy Cane

| DMC | X | BS |
|---|---|---|
| white | ⊡ | |
| 310 | | ╱ |
| 321 | | ╱ |
| 666 | ♥ | |
| 815 | ◪ | |
| 815 | | ╱ |
| 956 | I | |
| 989 | ◆ | |
| 3348 | H | |
| 3608 | ✚ | |

**24w x 34h** – Design stitched on 14 count white Aida using 3 strands for cross stitch, 1 strand for backstitching.

▱ Cutting line for Aida

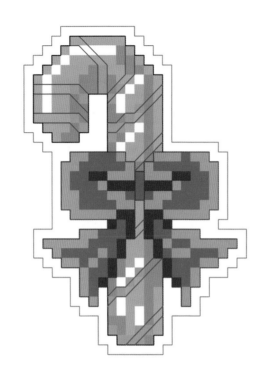

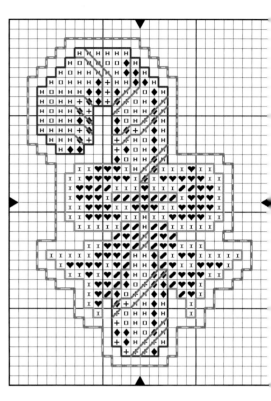

# Fair Isle Stocking

| DMC | X | 1/4 | BS | | DMC | X | 1/4 | BS |
|---|---|---|---|---|---|---|---|---|
| white | ⊡ | ⊡ | | | 797 | ■ | ◾ | |
| 310 | | | ╱ | | 797 | | | ╱ |
| 666 | ♥ | ♥ | | | 798 | ● | · | |
| 703 | L | L | | | 800 | H | H | |
| 742 | ★ | | | | 910 | ♣ | ♣ | |
| 743 | △ | | | | 970 | ✚ | ✚ | |

**30w x 36h** – Design stitched on 14 count white Aida using 3 strands for cross stitch, 1 strand for backstitching.

▱ Cutting line for Aida

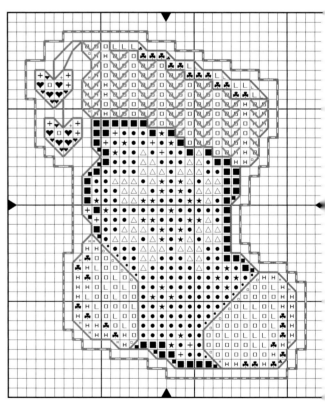

# House with Doll

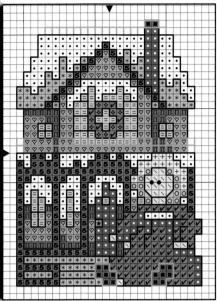

26w x 36h – Design stitched on 14 count white Aida using 3 strands for cross stitch, 1 strand for backstitching, 1 strand for French knots.

# Toy Store Sign

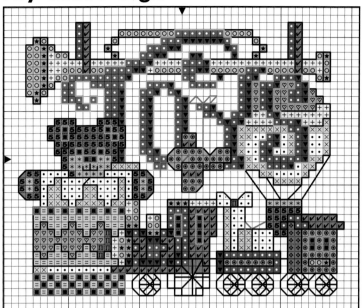

46w x 37h – Design stitched on 14 count white Aida using 3 strands for cross stitch, 1 strand for backstitching.

# House

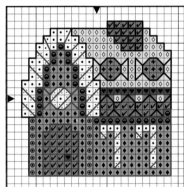

21w x 21h – Design stitched on 14 count white perforated plastic using 3 strands for cross stitch, 1 strand for backstitching.

# Bell

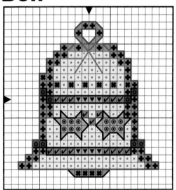

20w x 21h – Design stitched on 14 count white perforated plastic using 3 strands for cross stitch, 1 strand for backstitching.

# Angel

21w x 24h – Design stitched on 14 count white perforated plastic using 3 strands for cross stitch, 1 strand for backstitching.

| X | DMC | ¼X | B'ST |
|---|---|---|---|
| • | white | ◪ | |
| ◫ | 208 | | |
| ♡ | 210 | | |
| ■ | 310 | | ◪ |
| | 310 | | ◪ * |
| | 400 | | ◪ |
| ◆ | 402 | ◪ | |
| | 413 | | ◪ † |
| ∨ | 414 | | |
| ▽ | 518 | ◪ | |
| ◇ | 605 | ◪ | |
| ✔ | 666 | | ◪ |
| | 666 | | ◪ * |
| • | 676 | ▫ | |
| ▼ | 699 | | |
| ◉ | 702 | ◪ | |
| ▫ | 704 | | |
| ★ | 740 | | |
| ◯ | 742 | ◪ | |
| ✚ | 783 | ◪ | |
| ▼ | 796 | | |

| X | DMC | ¼X |
|---|---|---|
| ◖ | 798 | |
| ◉ | 814 | |
| ▣ | 815 | |
| 5 | 841 | ◪ |
| ✳ | 842 | |
| ∅ | 899 | |
| ◆ | 909 | |
| ◥ | 945 | ◪ |
| ✖ | 959 | ◪ |
| ◈ | 964 | ◪ |
| ▼ | 970 | |
| ✕ | 3072 | |
| ✛ | 3078 | |
| ✦ | 3607 | ◪ |
| ＝ | 3766 | |
| ◕ | 3776 | ◪ |
| • | 413 French Knot | |

\* Use **2** strands of floss.

† Use long stitches for balloon strings in Toy Store Sign.

15

# North Pole

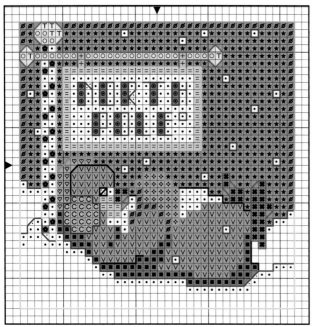

38w x 38h

# Sweet Dreams

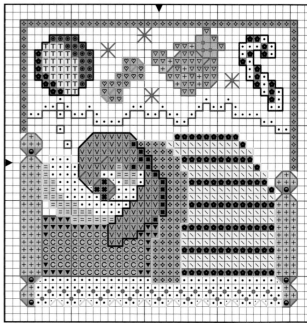

38w x 38h

# Skating

38w x 38h

# Building a Snowman

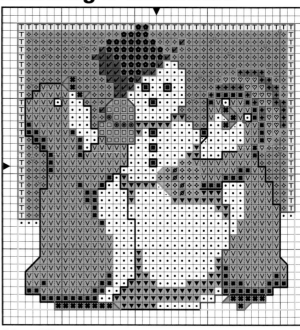

38w x 38h

Designs stitched on 14 count white Aida using 3 strands for cross stitch, 1 strand for backstitching, 1 strand for French knots.

| X | DMC | ¼X | B'ST |
|---|---|---|---|
| · | white | ◹ | ◹ * |
| ✔ | 304 | | ◹ |
| ■ | 310 | ◸ | ◹ |
| ∅ | 335 | ◸ | |
| ◖ | 400 | ◸ | ◹ * |
| + | 402 | ◸ | |
| ☒ | 415 | ◸ | |
| ⬠ | 666 | | |
| | 699 | | ◹ † |
| ◺ | 712 | ◻ | |
| ○ | 726 | ◸ | ◹ * |
| ◆ | 772 | | |
| ▼ | 775 | ◸ | |
| = | 776 | | |

| X | DMC | ¼X | B'ST |
|---|---|---|---|
| ◈ | 798 | ◸ | |
| | 820 | | ◹ † |
| ◉ | 911 | ◸ | |
| ▢ | 954 | ◸ | |
| ✖ | 977 | ◸ | |
| T | 3078 | ◻ | |
| ★ | 3325 | ◸ | |
| ✦ | 3326 | ◸ | |
| ◼ | 3607 | ◸ | |
| ♡ | 3609 | ◸ | |
| C | 3756 | ◸ | |
| V | 3799 | ◸ | |
| ▽ | 3827 | ◻ | |
| | | | ◹ |

| X | DMC | |
|---|---|---|
| ◉ | white | French Knot |
| ● | 310 | French Knot |
| ◉ | 400 | French Knot |

\* White for eyes. 726 and long stitches for stars. 400 for all other.

† 699 for wording, mitten, and hat. 820 for all other.

# Happy Santa

40w x 40h

# Santa with Moon

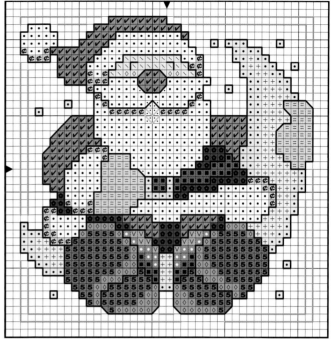

40w x40h

# Santa with Reindeer

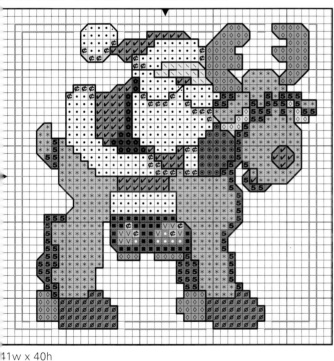

41w x 40h

# Merry Christmas

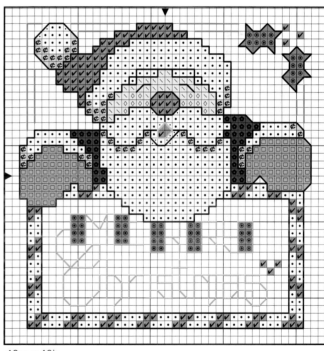

40w x 40h

Designs stitched on white 14 count white Aida using 3 strands for cross stitch, 1 strand for backstitching except where noted.

| X | DMC | 1/4X | B'ST | | X | DMC | 1/4X | B'ST |
|---|-----|------|------|---|---|-----|------|------|
| • | white | ◪ | | | • | 743 | | |
| ◈ | 300 | ◪ | | | + | 744 | ☐ | |
| ■ | 310 | ◪ | ◪ | | ⬢ | 815 | ◪ | ◪ |
| ▨ | 413 | ◪ | | | | 824 | | ◪* |
| V | 414 | | | | = | 825 | ☐ | |
| ¢ | 415 | ☐ | | | 5 | 841 | ◪ | |
| | 500 | | ◪ | | * | 842 | ◪ | |
| ◇ | 605 | ☐ | | | ＼ | 945 | ☐ | |
| ✔ | 666 | ◪ | ◪* | | ∅ | 3776 | ◪ | |
| ◉ | 699 | ◪ | ◪* | | | | | |
| ☐ | 704 | ◪ | | | * Use **2** strands of floss. | | | |

17

# Santa with Puppy

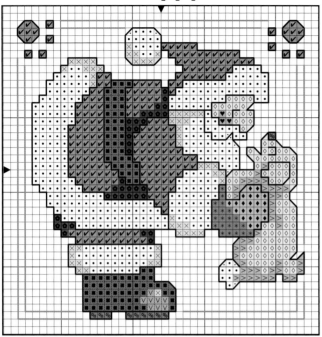

40w x 40h

# Santa with Bag

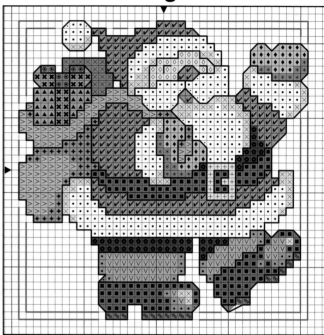

40w x 40h

# Santa with Bear

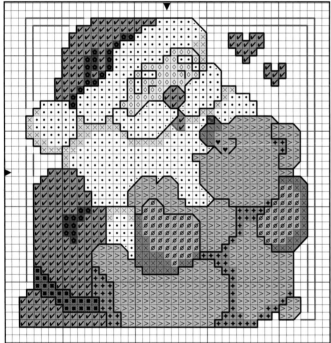

41w x 41h

# Santa on Rocking Horse

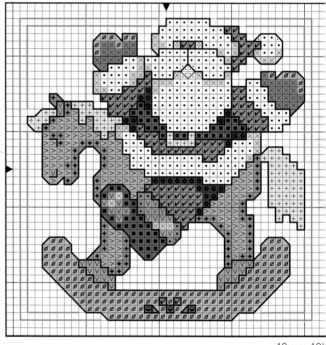

40w x 40h

Designs stitched on 14 count white
Aida using 3 strands for cross stitch,
1 strand for backstitching except
where noted.

| X | DMC | ¼X | B'ST | | X | DMC | ¼X | B'ST |
|---|-----|-----|------|---|---|-----|-----|------|
| • | white | ⌐ | | | ◙ | 815 | | ╱ |
| ‰ | 300 | ◣ | | | | 815 | | ╱* |
| ■ | 310 | ◣ | ╱ | | | 824 | | ╱* |
| > | 402 | ◣ | | | ✕ | 825 | ◣ | |
| • | 413 | ⌐ | | | ◣ | 842 | ◣ | |
| V | 414 | ◣ | | | ◇ | 945 | ◻ | |
| ✕ | 415 | ◻ | | | ✳ | 959 | ◣ | |
| ♥ | 605 | ◣ | | | ◆ | 964 | ◣ | |
| ✔ | 666 | ◣ | | | ◉ | 3607 | | |
| ◉ | 699 | ◣ | ╱* | | ✖ | 3609 | ◣ | |
| ▲ | 704 | ◣ | | | ✦ | 3776 | ◣ | |
| + | 743 | ◻ | | | | | | |
| ∅ | 813 | ◣ | | | | | | |

*Use **2** strands of floss.

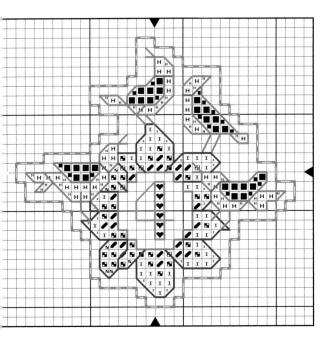

# Four Calling Birds

| DMC | X | 1/4 | BS | | DMC | X | 1/4 | BS |
|-----|---|-----|-----|---|-----|---|-----|-----|
| 310 | ■ | ◨ | | | 703 | ◪ | ◨ | |
| 310 | | | ╱ | | 815 | | | ╱ |
| 318 | H | H | | | 910 | ◗ | | |
| 666 | ♥ | | | | 910 | | | ╱ |
| 666 | | | ╱ | | 966 | ⊡ | ⊡ | |

**30w x 28h** – Design stitched on 14 count white Aida using 3 strands for cross stitch, 1 strand for backstitching.

✎ Cutting line for Aida

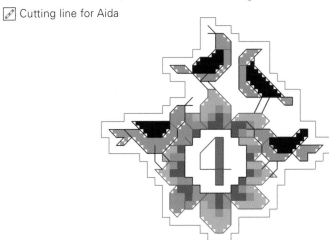

# Country Birdhouse

| DMC | X | 1/4 | BS | FK | | DMC | X | 1/4 |
|-----|---|-----|-----|-----|---|-----|---|-----|
| white | ⬚ | ⬚ | | | | 813 | H | H |
| 304 | ╱ | | | | | 909 | ◆ | |
| 310 | ■ | ◨ | | | | 912 | △ | |
| 310 | | | ╱ | ● | | 956 | ◥ | ◤ |
| 349 | ♥ | ♥ | | | | 975 | ◀ | ◁ |
| 369 | ⊡ | | | | | 3854 | ✚ | |
| 720 | ◉ | ◉ | | | | 3855 | T | |

**36w x 53h** – Design stitched on 14 count white Aida using 3 strands for cross stitch, 1 strand for backstitching, 1 strand for French knots.

✎ Cutting line for Aida

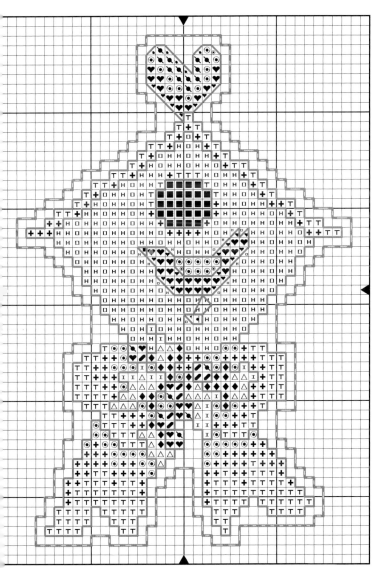

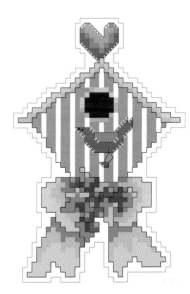

# Painting Santa

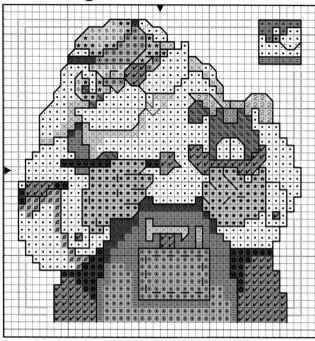

40w x 41h

# Santa's List

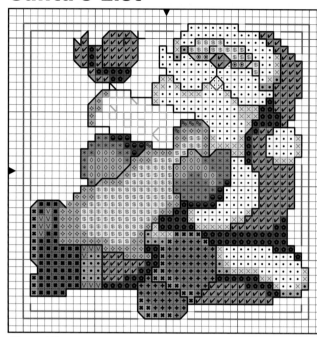

40w x 40h

# Skating Santa

40w x 40h

# Santa with Tree

43w x 41h

Designs stitched on 14 count white Aida using 3 strands for cross stitch and 1 strand for backstitching except where noted.

| X | DMC | ¼X | B'ST |
|---|-----|-----|------|
| • | white | ◩ | |
| ✖ | 300 | ◪ | |
| ■ | 310 | ◪ | ◩ |
| ✦ | 402 | ◪ | |
| V | 413 | ◪ | |
| • | 414 | ◪ | |
| ✕ | 415 | ◪ | |
| | 500 | | ◪ |
| ✔ | 666 | ◪ | ◪* |
| ■ | 699 | ◪ | ◪* |

| X | DMC | ¼X | B'ST |
|---|-----|-----|------|
| ✱ | 701 | ◪ | |
| ◇ | 704 | ◪ | |
| 2 | 743 | ◻ | |
| + | 744 | ◪ | |
| ★ | 758 | ◻ | |
| ◉ | 813 | ◪ | |
| ▣ | 815 | ◪ | ◪* |
| ▽ | 824 | ◪ | ◪* |
| = | 825 | ◪ | |
| ✚ | 841 | ◪ | |

| X | DMC | ¼X |
|---|-----|-----|
| $ | 945 | ◻ |
| ♥ | 959 | |
| ∅ | 964 | ◪ |
| 5 | 970 | ◪ |
| ▽ | 3607 | ◪ |
| T | 3609 | ◪ |
| ‰ | 3776 | ◪ |

*Use **2** strands of floss for borders and **1** strand for all other.

# Elf

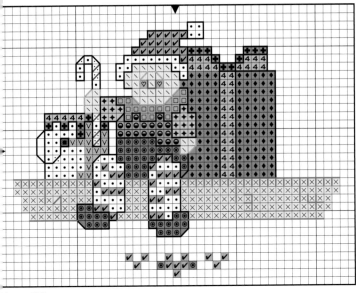

41w x 31h

# Sleigh

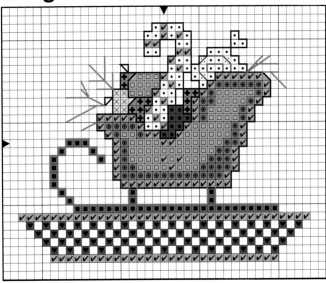

37w x 29h

# Train on Track

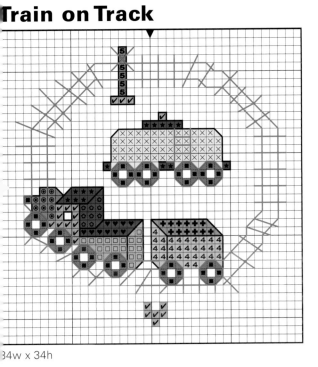

34w x 34h

# Santa with Tools

40w x 37h

Designs stitched on 14 count white Aida using 3 strands for cross stitch, 1 strand for backstitching except where noted.

| X | DMC | 1/4X | B'ST | | X | DMC | 1/4X | B'ST |
|---|-----|------|------|--|---|-----|------|------|
| • | white | ◩ | | | ◙ | 815 | ◩ | |
| ■ | 310 | ◩ | ◩ * | | ✳ | 898 | | ◩ † |
| | 355 | | ◩ | | + | 945 | | |
| 5 | 453 | ◩ | | | ✦ | 977 | ◩ | |
| | 535 | | ◩ | | ♡ | 3326 | ◩ | |
| ✔ | 666 | ◩ | ◩ † | | ✚ | 3607 | ◩ | |
| ▼ | 699 | ◩ | ◩ ★ | | 4 | 3609 | ◩ | |
| ◉ | 702 | ◩ | | | ◆ | 3766 | ◩ | |
| ▢ | 703 | ◩ | | | ◈ | 3779 | ◩ | |
| ◒ | 721 | ◩ | | | | | | |
| ⊠ | 725 | ▢ | | | | | | |
| ▨ | 754 | ▢ | | | | | | |
| V | 762 | ◩ | | | | | | |
| ★ | 798 | ◩ | | | | | | |
| ✴ | 809 | ◩ | | | | | | |

*Use **2** strands for train track and "X" on railroad sign and **1** strand for all other.

†666 for mouths, peppermint, and candy cane. 898 for Santa's eyes and mallet.

★Use **2** strands and long stitches.

# Painting Bear

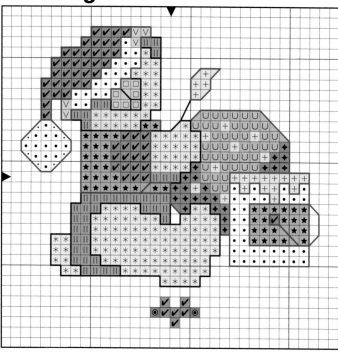

30w x 29h

# Bear with House

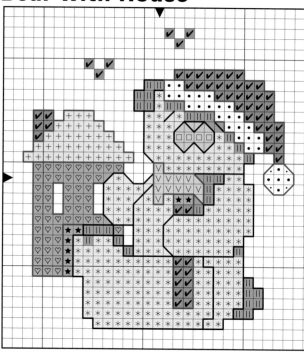

27w x 29h

# Paint Can Bear

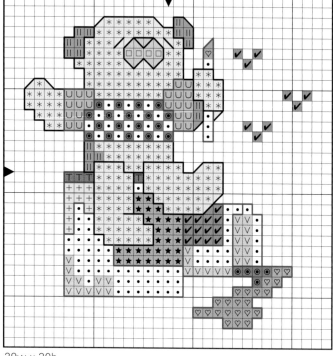

29w x 30h

Designs stitched on 14 count white Aida using 3 strands for cross stitch, 1 strand for backstitching.

# Rocking Horse

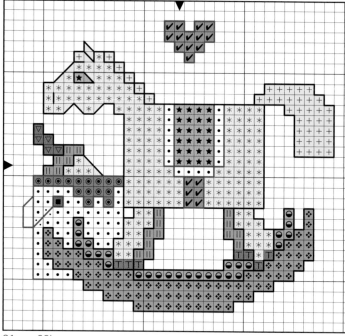

31w x 28h

| X | DMC | ¼X | B'ST | | X | DMC | ¼X | B'ST |
|---|---|---|---|---|---|---|---|---|
| · | white | ◿ | | | ⊡ | 738 | ◿ | |
| ■ | 310 | | | | ∨ | 762 | ◿ | |
| ‖ | 402 | ◿ | | | ★ | 798 | ◿ | |
| T | 453 | | | | | 898 | | ◿ |
| | 535 | | ◿ | | ▽ | 921 | | |
| ✔ | 666 | ◿ | | | ✳ | 945 | ⊡ | |
| ◉ | 702 | | | | ✧ | 977 | | |
| ♡ | 703 | ◿ | | | ✦ | 3607 | ◿ | |
| ◐ | 721 | | | | U | 3609 | ◿ | |
| + | 725 | ◻ | | | | | | |

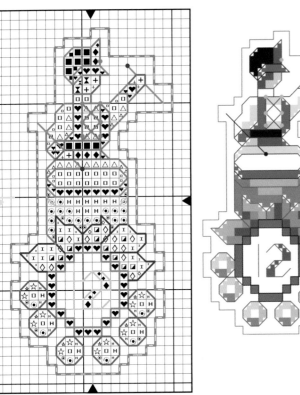

# Twelve Drummers Drumming

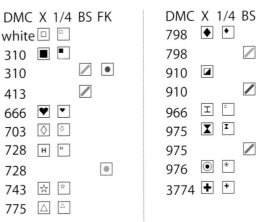

| DMC | X | 1/4 | BS | FK | | DMC | X | 1/4 | BS |
|-----|---|-----|----|----|--|-----|---|-----|----|
| white | □ | □ | | | | 798 | ◆ | ◆ | |
| 310 | ■ | ■ | | | | 798 | | | ╱ |
| 310 | | | ╱ | ● | | 910 | ◪ | | |
| 413 | | | ╱ | | | 910 | | | ╱ |
| 666 | ♥ | ♥ | | | | 966 | ⊞ | ⊞ | |
| 703 | ◇ | ◇ | | | | 975 | ✕ | ✕ | |
| 728 | H | H | | | | 975 | | | ╱ |
| 728 | | | | ● | | 976 | ◉ | ◉ | |
| 743 | ☆ | ☆ | | | | 3774 | ✚ | ✚ | |
| 775 | △ | △ | | | | | | | |

**18w x 37h** – Design stitched on 14 count white Aida using 3 strands for cross stitch, 1 strand for backstitching, 1 strand for French knots.

✂ Cutting line for Aida

# Six Geese A-laying

| DMC | X | 1/4 | BS | FK | | DMC | X | 1/4 | BS |
|-----|---|-----|----|----|--|-----|---|-----|----|
| white | □ | □ | | | | 798 | ╱ | ╱ | |
| 310 | | | ╱ | ● | | 800 | H | H | |
| 413 | | | ╱ | | | 975 | | | ╱ |
| 666 | ♥ | | | | | 3823 | ✚ | ✚ | |
| 742 | ▲ | ▲ | | | | | | | |

**34w x 28h** – Design stitched on 14 count white Aida using 3 strands for cross stitch, 1 strand for backstitching, 1 strand for French knots.

✂ Cutting line for Aida

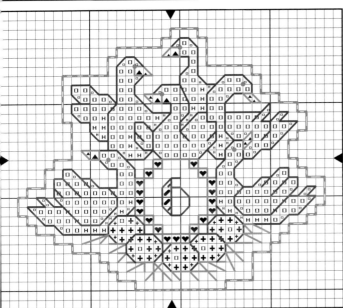

# Fruit Wreath

| DMC | X | 1/4 | BS | FK |
|-----|---|-----|----|----|
| 208 | ◆ | ◆ | | |
| 209 | L | L | | |
| 413 | | | ╱ | |
| 666 | | | | ● |
| 666 | ♥ | ♥ | | |
| 676 | ⊞ | ⊞ | | |
| 702 | ↑ | ↑ | | |
| 704 | ◇ | ◇ | | |
| 783 | ✕ | ✕ | | |
| 814 | ╱ | ╱ | | |
| 947 | △ | △ | | |

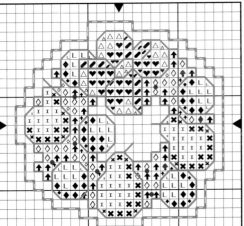

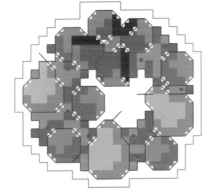

**23w x 22h** – Design stitched on 14 count white Aida using 3 strands for cross stitch, 1 strand for backstitching, 1 strand for French knots.

✂ Cutting line for Aida

# Tools

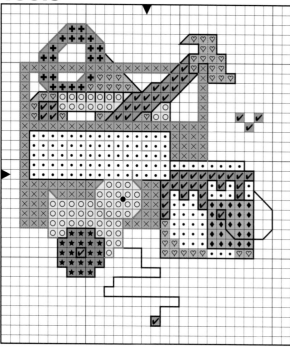

27w x 31h

# Santa's Workshop

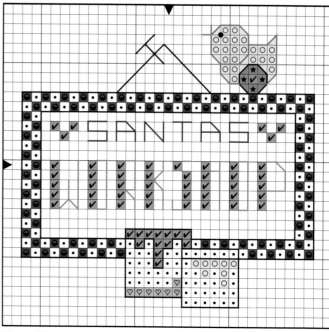

31w x 29h

# Train

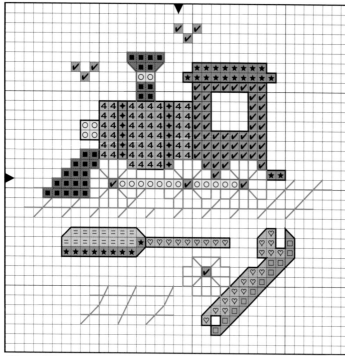

33w x 32h

# Station

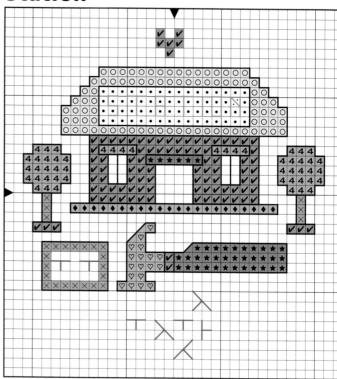

32w x 34h

Designs stitched on 14 count white
Aida using 3 strands for cross stitch,
1 strand for backstitching, 1 strand for
French knots except where noted.

| X | DMC | ¼X | B'ST |
|---|---|---|---|
| · | white | | |
| ■ | 310 | ◪ | ◪ |
| | 310 | | ◪* |
| ⊠ | 402 | ◪ | |
| ▢ | 453 | ◪ | |
| | 535 | | ◪ |
| ✔ | 666 | ◪ | ◪* |
| ◼ | 699 | | |
| ◆ | 702 | | |
| 4 | 703 | | |

| X | DMC | ¼X | B'ST |
|---|---|---|---|
| ✚ | 721 | | |
| ○ | 725 | ◪ | |
| ♡ | 762 | ◪ | |
| ★ | 798 | ◪ | ◪* |
| ⊟ | 809 | ◪ | |
| | 898 | | ◪ |
| ✚ | 921 | ◪ | |
| ● | 898 French Knot | | |

*Use **2** strands for Train and Santa's
Workshop.

# Santa's Bake Shop

46w x 35h

# Cookie House

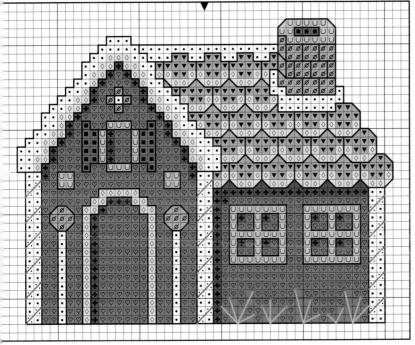

46w x 36h

# Sweet Treats

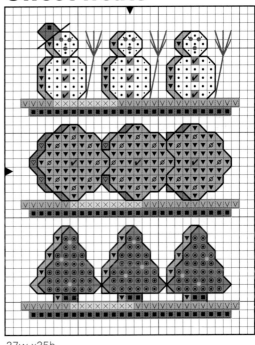

27w x35h

Designs stitched on 14 count ivory Aida using 3 strands for cross stitch, 1 strand for backstitching, 1 strand for French knots except where noted.

| X | DMC | 1/4X | B'ST |
|---|------|------|------|
| • | white | ◢ | |
| | 310 | | ◿ |
| V | 415 | ◢ | |
| ✚ | 434 | ◢ | |
| ♥ | 435 | ◢ | |
| ▼ | 437 | ◢ | |
| ■ | 535 | ◢ | |
| ⌀ | 602 | ◢ | |
| ◇ | 605 | ◻ | |
| ✔ | 666 | | ◿ * |
| ✤ | 738 | ◢ | |
| ✕ | 762 | ◻ | |
| U | 775 | ◢ | |

| X | DMC | 1/4X | B'ST |
|---|------|------|------|
| ◉ | 913 | ◢ | ◿ † |
| | 938 | | ◿ |
| | 938 | | ◿ ★ |
| • | white | | French Knot |
| • | 602 | | French Knot |
| • | 666 | | French Knot |
| • | 744 | | French Knot |
| • | 938 | | French Knot |

* Use **2** strands for Santa's Bake Shop. Use 1 strand and long stitches for Cookie House.
† Use long stitches.
★ Use 2 strands and long stitches.

25

# Silly Snowman

| DMC | X | 1/4 | BS | FK |
|-----|---|-----|----|----|
| white | ▢ | ▢ | | |
| 310 | ■ | ■ | | |
| 310 | | | ╱ | ● |
| 400 | ✖ | ✖ | | |
| 413 | | | ╱ | |
| 553 | ⊥ | | | |
| 666 | ♥ | ♥ | | |

| DMC | X | 1/4 | BS | FK |
|-----|---|-----|----|----|
| 666 | | | | ╱ |
| 703 | ◣ | ◢ | | |
| 741 | ◪ | ◪ | | |
| 775 | △ | | | |
| 956 | H | | | |
| 963 | L | L | | |

**34w x 36h –** Design stitched on 14 count white Aida using 3 strands for cross stitch, 1 strand for backstitching, 1 strand for French knots.

╱ Cutting line for Aida

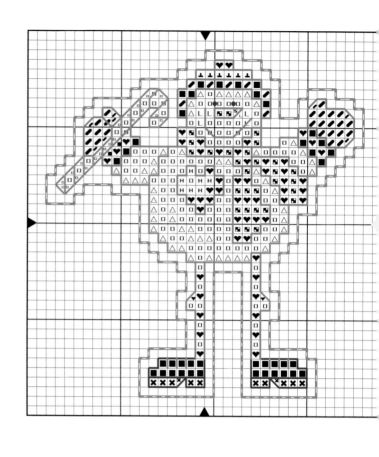

# Gingerbread Man Cookie

| DMC | X | 1/4 | BS | FK |
|-----|---|-----|----|----|
| white | | | ╱ | |
| 310 | | | ╱ | ● |
| 400 | ◣ | | | |
| 400 | | | ╱ | |
| 402 | H | H | | |
| 666 | ♥ | ♥ | | |
| 815 | ◆ | | | |
| 815 | | | ╱ | |
| 3776 | ✖ | ✖ | | |

**15w x 17h –** Design stitched on 14 count white Aida using 3 strands for cross stitch, 1 strand for backstitching, 1 strand for French knots.

╱ Cutting line for Aida

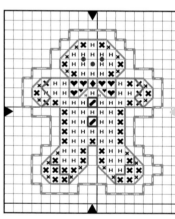

# Happy Holidays Sign

| DMC | X | 1/4 | BS | FK |
|-----|---|-----|----|----|
| white | ▢ | | | |
| 310 | | | ╱ | |
| 608 | H | H | | |
| 666 | ♥ | | | |
| 666 | | | | ● |
| 703 | Z | Z | | |
| 783 | | | ╱ | |
| 815 | ◣ | ◢ | | |
| 910 | ◆ | | | |
| 966 | L | L | | |

**29w x 22h –** Design stitched on 14 count white Aida using 3 strands for cross stitch, 1 strand for backstitching, 1 strand for French knots.

╱ Cutting line for Aida

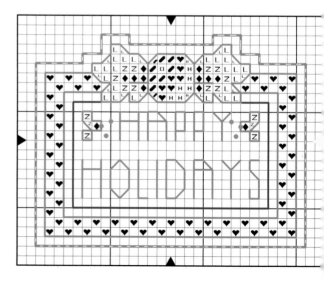

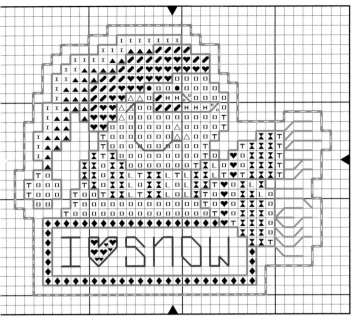

# I Love Snow

| DMC | X | 1/4 | BS | FK | DMC | X | 1/4 | BS |
|-----|---|-----|----|----|-----|---|-----|----|
| white | ▣ | ▫ | | | 741 | H | ᴴ | |
| 208 | ▲ | | | | 798 | ☒ | | |
| 210 | I | | | | 809 | L | | |
| 310 | | | ◥ | ● | 815 | | | ◥ |
| 413 | | | ◥ | | 963 | △ | | |
| 666 | ♥ | ♥ | | | 970 | ◪ | | |
| 666 | | | ◥ | | 3753 | T | | |
| 703 | ◆ | | | | | | | |

**34w x 28h** – Design stitched on 14 count white Aida using 3 strands for cross stitch, 1 strand for backstitching, 1 strand for French knots.

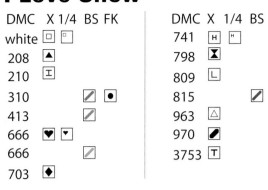

🖉 Cutting line for Aida

**26w x 44h** – Design stitched on 14 count white Aida using 3 strands for cross stitch, 1 strand for backstitching, 1 strand for French knots.

🖉 Cutting line for Aida

# Jack-in-the-Box

| DMC | X | 1/4 | BS | FK |
|-----|---|-----|----|----|
| white | ▣ | ▫ | | |
| 208 | ☒ | ᴵ | | |
| 210 | T | ᵀ | | |
| 310 | ■ | ▪ | | |
| 310 | | | ◥ | ● |
| 413 | | | ◥ | |
| 415 | I | | | |
| 666 | ♥ | | | |
| 666 | | | ◥ | |
| 703 | ✚ | ✛ | | |
| 725 | ◖ | ◤ | | |
| 727 | H | ᴴ | | |
| 815 | ◥ | ◢ | | |
| 911 | ◆ | | | |
| 920 | | ◂ | | |
| 920 | | | ◥ | |
| 947 | ▲ | | | |
| 948 | L | ᴸ | | |
| 956 | ⬆ | ⬆ | | |
| 957 | Z | | | |

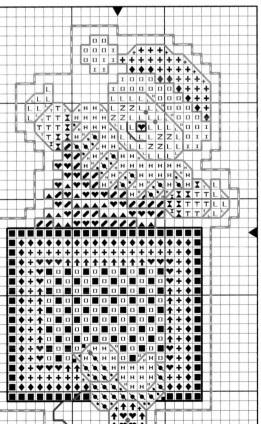

27

# Five Golden Rings

| DMC | X | 1/4 | BS |
|---|---|---|---|
| white | ▣ | ▫ | |
| 310 | | | ╱ |
| 413 | | | ╱ |
| 666 | ♥ | ♥ | |
| 676 | ✖ | ✖ | |
| 703 | △ | △ | |
| 809 | ⚓ | ⚓ | |
| 910 | ■ | ■ | |
| 910 | | | ╱ |
| 966 | H | H | |
| 975 | | | ╱ |
| 3823 | L | L | |

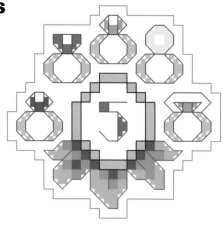

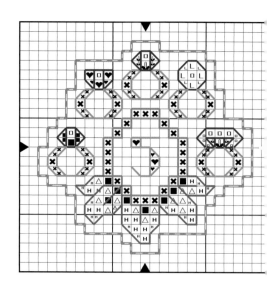

**23w x 22h** – Design stitched on 14 count white Aida using 3 strands for cross stitch, 1 strand for backstitching.

✐ Cutting line for Aida

# Red Ornament

| DMC | X | 1/4 | BS |
|---|---|---|---|
| white | ▣ | | |
| 310 | | | ╱ |
| 498 | ◨ | ◨ | |
| 498 | | | ╱ |
| 608 | H | H | |
| 666 | ♥ | ♥ | |
| 703 | ✚ | ✚ | |
| 742 | Z | Z | |
| 800 | ◣ | ◣ | |
| 910 | ◆ | | |
| 956 | ⬆ | | |
| 957 | I | | |
| 966 | L | L | |

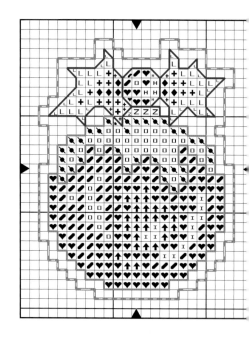

21w x 27h – Design stitched on 14 count white Aida using 3 strands for cross stitch, 1 strand for backstitching.

✐ Cutting line for Aida

# Three French Hens

| DMC | X | 1/4 | BS | FK |
|---|---|---|---|---|
| 310 | | | ╱ | ● |
| 317 | | | ╱ | |
| 435 | ◨ | | | |
| 437 | ★ | ★ | | |
| 666 | ♥ | ♥ | | |
| 703 | ▲ | ▲ | | |
| 798 | ◆ | ◆ | | |
| 798 | | | ╱ | |
| 922 | ✖ | | | |
| 951 | H | H | | |
| 975 | ■ | ■ | | |
| 975 | | | ╱ | |

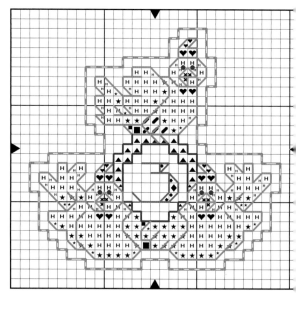

27w x 25h – Design stitched on 14 count white Aida using 3 strands for cross stitch, 1 strand for backstitching, 1 strand for French knots.

✐ Cutting line for Aida

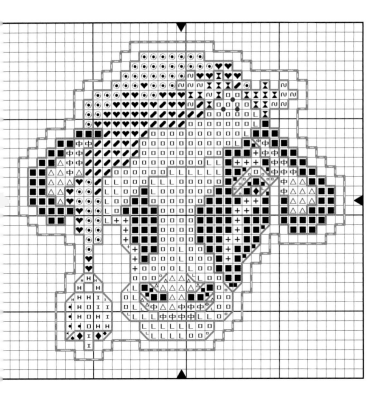

**35w x 33h** – Design stitched on 14 count white Aida using 3 strands for cross stitch, 1 strand for backstitching, 1 strand for French knots.

Cutting line for Aida

# Christmas Cow

| DMC | X | 1/4 | BS | FK | | DMC | X | 1/4 |
|-----|---|-----|----|----|----|-----|---|-----|
| white | ▢ | ▢ | | | | 783 | ◄ | ◄ |
| 310 | ■ | ■ | | | | 816 | ╱ | |
| 310 | | | ╱ | | | 818 | △ | △ |
| 414 | ✚ | ✚ | | | | 921 | ◆ | ◆ |
| 666 | ♥ | | | | | 946 | ◉ | |
| 666 | | | | ● | | 972 | H | H |
| 702 | ✗ | | | | | 3326 | ⊞ | ⊕ |
| 704 | ∾ | | | | | 3756 | L | L |
| 727 | I | I | | | | | | |

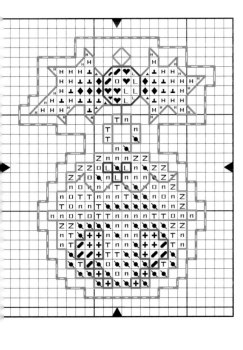

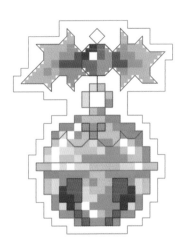

**21w x 27h** – Design stitched on 14 count white Aida using 3 strands for cross stitch, 1 strand for backstitching.

Cutting line for Aida

# Jingle Bell

| DMC | X | 1/4 | BS |
|-----|---|-----|----|
| white | ▢ | | |
| 608 | L | L | |
| 666 | ♥ | ♥ | |
| 703 | ⊥ | ⊥ | |
| 728 | n | | |
| 744 | T | | |
| 783 | ◥ | | |
| 815 | ╱ | ╱ | |
| 815 | | | ╱ |
| 910 | ◆ | | |
| 910 | | | ╱ |
| 920 | ✚ | | |
| 920 | | | ╱ |
| 966 | H | H | |
| 3776 | Z | | |
| 3799 | | | ╱ |

# Flying Santa

| DMC | X | 1/4 | BS | FK |
|---|---|---|---|---|
| white | □ | □ | | |
| 304 | ◩ | | | |
| 310 | ■ | ■ | | |
| 351 | H | H | | |
| 647 | L | | | |
| 666 | ♥ | ♥ | | |
| 666 | | | | ● |
| 676 | ✚ | + | | |
| 703 | △ | | | |
| 729 | ◆ | ◆ | | |
| 844 | ↑ | | | |
| 844 | | | ◪ | |
| 902 | ✖ | × | | |
| 902 | | | ◪ | |
| 911 | Z | | | |
| 911 | | | ◪ | |
| 945 | I | I | | |
| 3072 | o | o | | |

**37w x 27h** – Design stitched on 14 count white Aida using 3 strands for cross stitch, 1 strand for backstitching, 1 strand for French knots.

◪ Cutting line for Aida

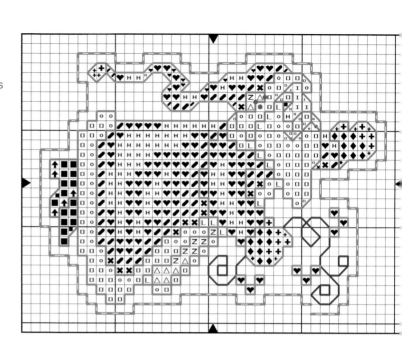

# Christmas Fox

| DMC | X | 1/4 | BS | FK |
|---|---|---|---|---|
| white | □ | □ | | |
| 310 | ■ | ■ | | |
| 310 | | | ◪ | ● |
| 402 | Z | z | | |
| 414 | ↓ | + | | |
| 648 | n | n | | |
| 666 | ♥ | | | |
| 702 | I | | | |
| 738 | ◊ | ◊ | | |

| DMC | X | 1/4 |
|---|---|---|
| 742 | 4 | 4 |
| 762 | ▲ | ▲ |
| 816 | ◩ | |
| 910 | ◆ | |
| 919 | ◥ | ◥ |
| 921 | ✖ | I |
| 946 | V | |
| 3756 | T | |

**33w x 32h** – Design stitched on 14 count white Aida using 3 strands for cross stitch, 1 strand for backstitching, 1 strand for French knots.

◪ Cutting line for Aida

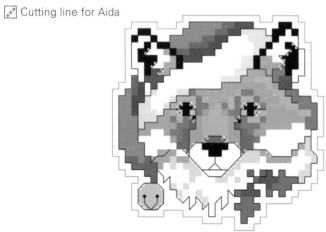

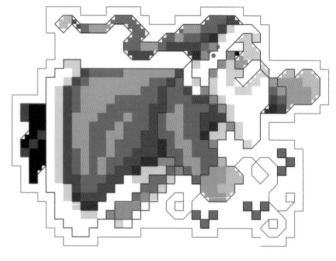

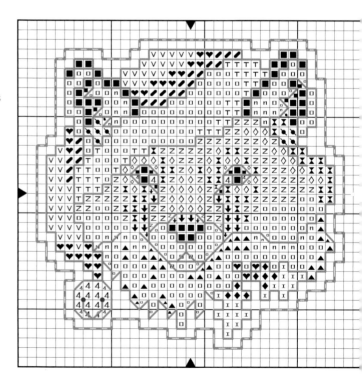

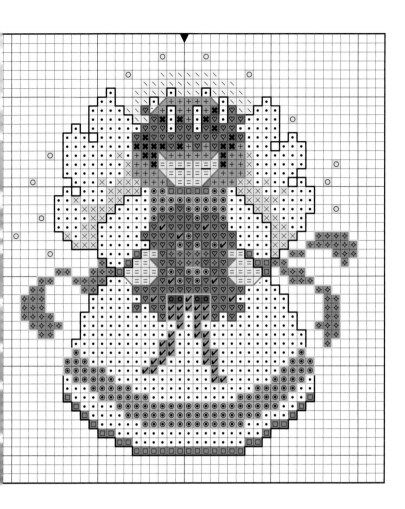

# Angel with Wreath

| X | DMC | ¼X | B'ST |
|---|---|---|---|
| • | white | ◹ | |
| + | 402 | ◹ | |
| | 413 | | ◿ |
| ⊠ | 415 | | |
| ✔ | 666 | | |
| ♡ | 701 | ◹ | |
| ◎ | 725 | | |
| ◉ | 815 | | ◹ |
| | 920 | | ◹ |
| = | 948 | ◻ | |
| | 986 | | ◿ |
| ▣ | 996 | ◹ | |
| ◹ | 3078 | ◻ | |
| ◉ | 3326 | | |
| ✧ | 3608 | | |
| ✖ | 3776 | | |

**40w x 45h –** Design stitched on 14 count white Aida using 3 strands for cross stitch, 1 strand for backstitching.

# Bear on Rocking Horse

| X | DMC | ¼X | B'ST |
|---|---|---|---|
| • | white | ◹ | |
| + | 402 | | |
| | 413 | | ◿ |
| ∨ | 414 | | |
| ⊠ | 415 | ◻ | |
| ✔ | 666 | | |
| ♡ | 701 | | |
| % | 704 | | |
| ◎ | 725 | | |
| | 815 | | ◹ |
| 4 | 838 | | ◹ |
| | 920 | | ◹ |
| | 986 | | ◹ |
| ✧ | 3608 | | |
| ✖ | 3776 | | |

**39w x 46h –** Design stitched on 14 count white Aida using 3 strands for cross stitch, 1 strand for backstitching.

# Nine Ladies Dancing

| DMC | X | 1/4 | BS | FK |
|-----|---|-----|----|----|
| white | | | | ● |
| 310 | ■ | ■ | | |
| 310 | | | ╱ | |
| 413 | | | ╱ | |
| 666 | ♥ | ♥ | | |
| 703 | ◇ | ◇ | | |
| 910 | ◆ | ◆ | | |
| 910 | | | ╱ | |
| 956 | ✚ | ✚ | | |
| 956 | | | ╱ | |
| 957 | H | H | | |
| 966 | T | T | | |
| 975 | ⬚ | ⬚ | | |
| 975 | | | ╱ | |
| 3774 | I | I | | |

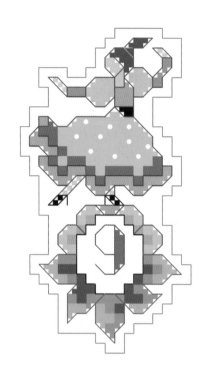

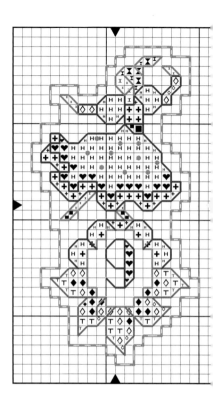

**18w x 33h –** Design stitched on 14 count white Aida using 3 strands for cross stitch, 1 strand for backstitching, 1 strand for French knots.

✏ Cutting line for Aida

# Meowy Christmas

| DMC | X | 1/4 | BS | FK |
|-----|---|-----|----|----|
| white | □ | □ | | |
| 310 | ■ | | | |
| 310 | | | ╱ | |
| 415 | H | | | |
| 666 | ♥ | ♥ | | |
| 666 | | | | ● |
| 703 | ◣ | | | |
| 721 | ✚ | ✚ | | |
| 722 | Z | Z | | |
| 815 | ◢ | ◢ | | |
| 815 | | | ╱ | |
| 910 | ◆ | | | |
| 921 | ⊥ | | | |
| 956 | ⬆ | ⬆ | | |
| 966 | I | I | | |
| 3825 | T | T | | |

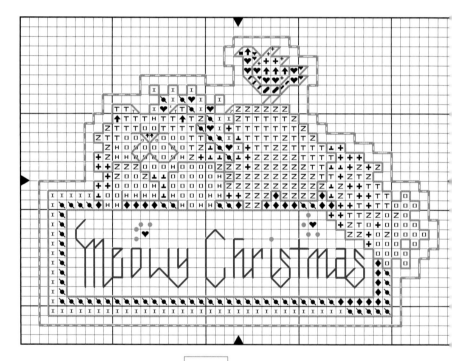

**43w x 30h –** Design stitched on 14 count white Aida using 3 strands for cross stitch, 1 strand for backstitching, 1 strand for French knots.

✏ Cutting line for Aida

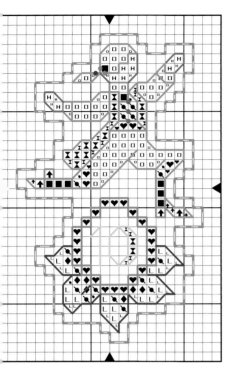
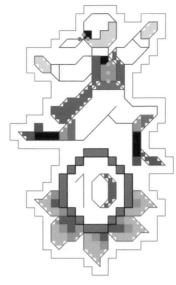

# Ten Lords A-leaping

| DMC | X | 1/4 | BS | FK |
|-----|---|-----|----|----|
| white | ▢ | ▢ | | |
| 310 | ■ | | | |
| 310 | | | ◲ | |
| 413 | | | ◲ | |
| 666 | ♥ | ♥ | | |
| 666 | | | | ● |
| 703 | ◣ | ◤ | | |
| 703 | | | | ● |
| 728 | | | | ● |
| 798 | ✖ | ✚ | | |
| 798 | | | ◲ | |
| 910 | ◆ | | | |
| 910 | | | ◲ | |
| 966 | L | L | | |
| 975 | ⬆ | ⬆ | | |
| 975 | | | ◲ | |
| 3774 | H | H | | |

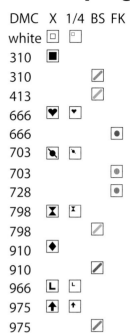

**20w x 32h** – Design stitched on 14 count white Aida using 3 strands for cross stitch, 1 strand for backstitching, 1 strand for French knots.

✎ Cutting line for Aida

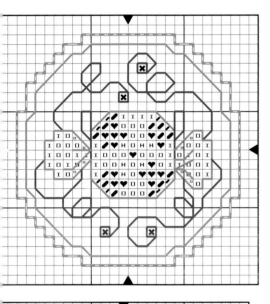
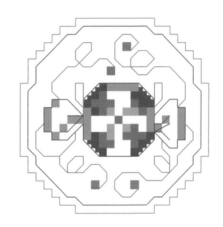

# Peppermint Candy

| DMC | X | 1/4 | BS |
|-----|---|-----|----|
| white | ▢ | ▢ | |
| 351 | H | | |
| 304 | ◕ | | ◲ |
| 666 | ♥ | | |
| 647 | I | | |
| 844 | | | ◲ |
| 911 | ✖ | | |
| 911 | | | ◲ |

**24w x 24h** – Design stitched on 14 count white Aida using 3 strands for cross stitch, 1 strand for backstitching.

✎ Cutting line for Aida

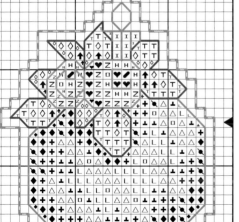

# Lavender Ornament

| DMC | X | 1/4 | BS | DMC | X | 1/4 | BS |
|-----|---|-----|----|-----|---|-----|----|
| white | ▢ | | | 815 | | | ◲ |
| 208 | ✚ | ✛ | | 910 | ⬆ | ⬆ | |
| 209 | ◪ | ◪ | | 910 | | | ◲ |
| 210 | L | L | | 946 | ♥ | ♥ | |
| 327 | ◆ | ◆ | | 966 | T | T | |
| 327 | | | ◲ | 970 | Z | Z | |
| 415 | I | I | | 972 | H | H | |
| 703 | ◇ | ◇ | | 3844 | ◣ | | |
| 815 | ◲ | | | 3846 | △ | | |

**23w x 27h** – Design stitched on 14 count white Aida using 3 strands for cross stitch, 1 strand for backstitching.

✎ Cutting line for Aida

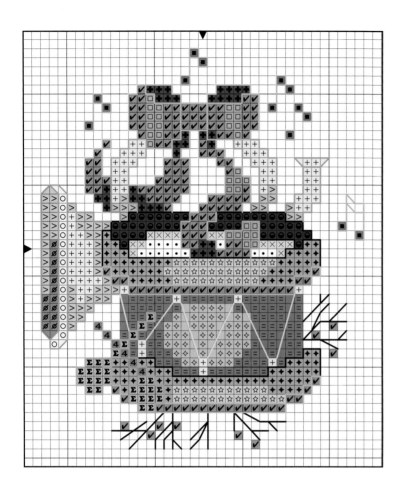

## Drum

| X | DMC | ¼X | B'ST |
|---|---|---|---|
| • | white | | |
| ■ | 310 | | ◹* |
| ✕ | 415 | | |
| ✔ | 666 | | |
| ◕ | 699 | | |
| ✦ | 704 | | |
| + | 725 | ☐ | ◹† |
| ☆ | 772 | | |
| > | 783 | ◹ | |
| ◈ | 798 | | |
| ✚ | 815 | | ◹ |
| = | 820 | | |
| | 838 | | ◹* |
| 4 | 839 | | |
| Σ | 841 | | |
| ∅ | 920 | ◹ | ◹ |
| ☐ | 947 | | |
| | 986 | | ◹ |
| ◎ | 3078 | ☐ | |

\*310 for musical notes. 838 for
drumsticks.
†Use **2** strands for long stitches.

**37w x 44h –** Design stitched on 14 count white Aida
using 3 strands for cross stitch, 1 strand for backstitching
except where noted.

## Santa in Chimney

| X | DMC | ¼X | B'ST |
|---|---|---|---|
| • | white | ◹ | |
| ● | 413 | | ◹ |
| V | 414 | ◹ | |
| ✕ | 415 | ◹ | |
| ✔ | 666 | | |
| ☆ | 701 | | |
| + | 725 | ☐ | |
| ◈ | 798 | ◹ | |
| ✚ | 815 | ◹ | ◹ |
| % | 838 | | ◹ |
| 4 | 839 | | |
| Σ | 841 | | |
| | 920 | | ◹ |
| ◆ | 945 | ◹ | |
| ☐ | 947 | ◹ | |
| | 948 | ☐ | |
| ✖ | 986 | | ◹ |
| ◉ | 996 | ◹ | |
| ○ | 3078 | | |
| ★ | 3326 | ◹ | |
| 2 | 3608 | ◹ | |

**42w x 49h –** Design stitched on 14 count white
Aida using 3 strands for cross stitch, 1 strand for
backstitching.

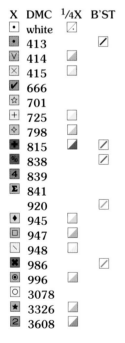

# Merry Christmas

| X | DMC | 1/4X | B'ST |
|---|-----|------|------|
| • | white | | |
| | 413 | ☑ | |
| ✔ | 666 | | |
| ◕ | 699 | | |
| ▼ | 701 | ◩ | |
| ◈ | 704 | | |
| ❽ | 725 | ◩ | |
| + | 783 | ◩ | |
| ◕ | 815 | | ☑ |
| | 920 | | ☑* |
| | 986 | | ☑ |
| 4 | 3078 | ☐ | |

*Use **2** strands for "Merry Christmas" and 1 strand for all other.
Note: Backstitch year using **2** strands 666.

9w x 48h – Design stitched on 14 count white Aida using strands for cross stitch, 1 strand for backstitching except where noted.

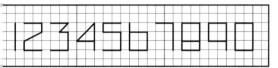

center year

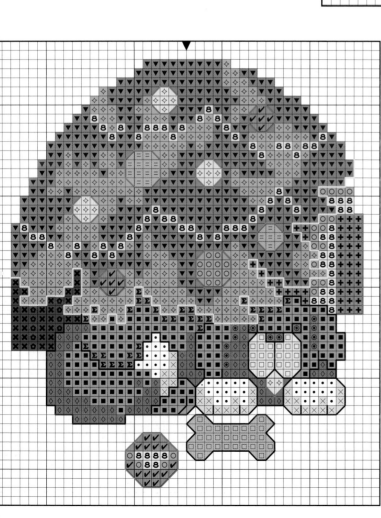

# Puppy Under Tree

| X | DMC | 1/4X | B'ST |
|---|-----|------|------|
| • | white | ◩ | |
| ■ | 402 | ◩ | ☑ |
| | 413 | | ☑ |
| ⊠ | 415 | ☐ | |
| ✔ | 666 | ◩ | |
| ▼ | 699 | ◩ | |
| ◈ | 701 | ☐ | |
| ❽ | 725 | | |
| ◕ | 815 | | ☑ |
| ✖ | 820 | | |
| ◉ | 838 | | ☑ |
| ☐ | 841 | ◩ | |
| Σ | 920 | | |
| ☐ | 945 | ☐ | |
| ○ | 947 | ◩ | |
| | 986 | | ☐ |
| = | 996 | ◩ | |
| ◈ | 3326 | ☐ | |
| + | 3608 | | |
| ◈ | 3776 | ◩ | |

40w x 47h – Design stitched on 14 count white Aida using 3 strands for cross stitch, 1 strand for backstitching.

35

# North Pole

| DMC | X | 1/4 | BS |
|-----|---|-----|-----|
| white | ▫ | | |
| 310 | ■ | | |
| 310 | | | ╱ |
| 453 | L | | |
| 666 | ♥ | ♥ | |
| 703 | T | | |
| 720 | ◆ | ◆ | |
| 742 | ✖ | ✖ | |
| 743 | H | H | |
| 815 | ╱ | ╱ | |
| 815 | | | ╱ |
| 910 | ⬆ | | |
| 910 | | | ╱ |
| 970 | ✚ | ✚ | |

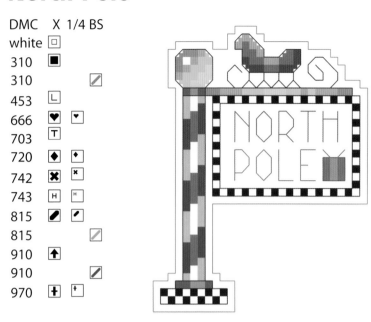

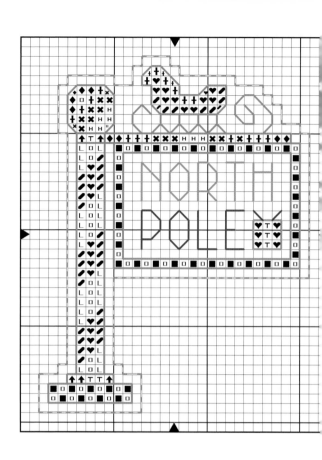

**29w x 37h** – Design stitched on 14 count white Aida using 3 strands for cross stitch, 1 strand for backstitching.

✎ Cutting line for Aida

# Polar Bear

| DMC | X | 1/4 | BS | FK |
|-----|---|-----|-----|-----|
| white | ▫ | ▫ | | |
| 310 | ■ | ■ | | |
| 310 | | | ╱ | ● |
| 413 | | | ╱ | |
| 498 | ╱ | | | |
| 666 | ♥ | | | |
| 703 | ⬆ | | | |
| 742 | H | | | |

| DMC | X | 1/4 | BS |
|-----|---|-----|-----|
| 809 | ◆ | | |
| 945 | I | I | |
| 957 | Z | | |
| 975 | | ▲ | |
| 975 | | | ╱ |
| 977 | ✚ | ✚ | |
| 3753 | L | L | |
| 3827 | T | T | |

**32w x 36h** – Design stitched on 14 count white Aida using 3 strands for cross stitch, 1 strand for backstitching, 1 strand for French knot.

✎ Cutting line for Aida

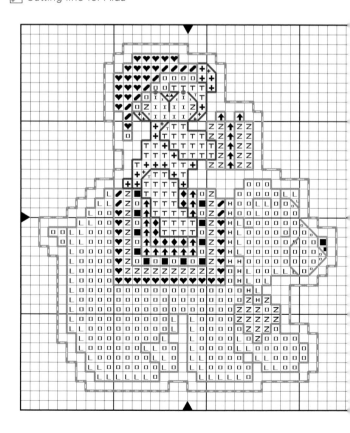

# Eight Maids A-milking

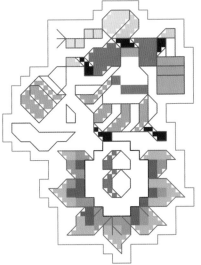

| DMC | X | 1/4 | BS |
|---|---|---|---|
| white | ▣ | ▫ | |
| 310 | ■ | ▪ | |
| 310 | | | ╱ |
| 413 | | | ╱ |
| 666 | ♥ | ♥ | |
| 703 | ◣ | ◥ | |
| 744 | H | H | |
| 809 | T | T | |
| 910 | ◆ | ◆ | |
| 910 | | | ╱ |
| 966 | I | I | |
| 975 | | | ╱ |
| 3773 | ✚ | + | |
| 3774 | L | L | |

**21w x 28h –** Design stitched on 14 count White Aida using 3 strands for cross stitch, 1 strand for backstitching.

▱ Cutting line for Aida

# Ornament Wreath

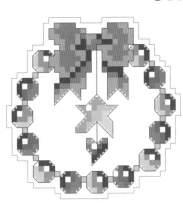

| DMC | X | 1/4 | BS |
|---|---|---|---|
| white | ▣ | | |
| 400 | | | ╱ |
| 369 | H | H | |
| 500 | | | ╱ |
| 606 | ✚ | + | |
| 666 | ♥ | ♥ | |
| 703 | ◣ | ◥ | |
| 742 | L | L | |
| 743 | T | T | |
| 815 | ◢ | ◢ | |
| 815 | | | ╱ |
| 909 | ◆ | ◆ | |
| 970 | ⬆ | ⬆ | |

**33w x 33h –** Design stitched on 14 count white Aida using 3 strands for cross stitch, 1 strand for backstitching.

▱ Cutting line for Aida

# Panda

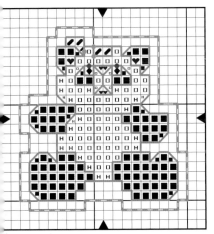

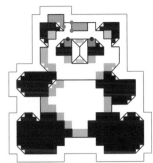

| DMC | X | 1/4 | BS | FK |
|---|---|---|---|---|
| white | ▣ | ▫ | | |
| 310 | ■ | ▪ | | |
| 310 | | | ╱ | ● |
| 334 | ◆ | | | |
| 648 | H | H | | |
| 666 | | | | ● |
| 704 | ◢ | ◢ | | |
| 3326 | ♥ | ♥ | | |

**18w x 19h –** Design stitched on 14 count white Aida using 3 strands for cross stitch, 1 strand for backstitching, 1 strand for French knots.

▱ Cutting line for Aida

37

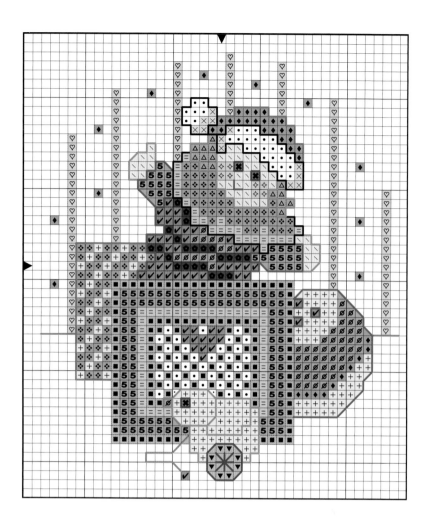

## Toys

| X | DMC | 1/4X | B'ST |
|---|---|---|---|
| • | white | · | |
| ■ | 310 | | ⁄ |
| | 413 | | ⁄ |
| ⊠ | 415 | | |
| ✔ | 666 | | |
| ◆ | 701 | �￼ | |
| ♡ | 704 | | |
| + | 725 | ◻ | |
| △ | 783 | | |
| ❖ | 798 | | |
| ⬠ | 815 | | ⁄ |
| ✹ | 838 | | ⁄ |
| ▼ | 841 | ◻ | |
| | 920 | | ⁄ |
| ∅ | 947 | ◻ | |
| ＼ | 948 | ◻ | |
| | 986 | | ⁄ |
| = | 996 | | |
| ❖ | 3326 | | |
| 5 | 3608 | ◻ | |

**41w x 47h** – Design stitched on 14 count white Aida using 3 strands for cross stitch, 1 strand for backstitching.

# Santa with Presents

| X | DMC | 1/4X | B'ST |
|---|---|---|---|
| • | white | · | |
| ✚ | 402 | ◻ | |
| | 413 | | ⁄ |
| ⊠ | 415 | ◻ | |
| ✔ | 666 | | |
| ◆ | 701 | | |
| ♡ | 704 | | |
| + | 725 | | |
| ⬠ | 815 | | ⁄ |
| ❖ | 820 | | |
| ✹ | 838 | | ⁄ |
| ▼ | 841 | | |
| | 920 | | ⁄ |
| ◻ | 945 | ◻ | |
| ∅ | 947 | | |
| ＼ | 948 | ◻ | |
| ⬠ | 986 | | ⁄ |
| = | 996 | | |
| ❖ | 3326 | ◻ | |
| 5 | 3608 | | |

**42w x 46h** – Design stitched on 14 count white Aida using 3 strands for cross stitch, 1 strand for backstitching.

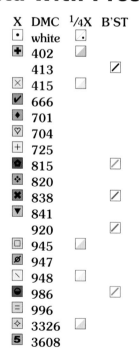

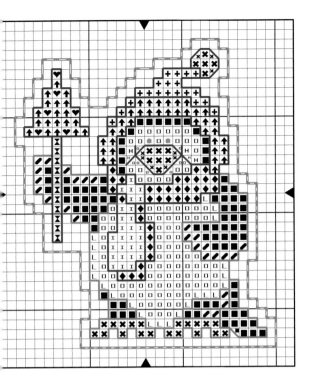

# Chilly Penguin

| DMC | X | 1/4 | BS | FK |     | DMC | X | 1/4 |
|-----|---|-----|----|----|-----|-----|---|-----|
| white | ☐ | ☐ | | | | 741 | ✖ | ✶ |
| 310 | ■ | ▪ | | | | 963 | H | H |
| 310 | | | ╱ | ● | | 3607 | ◆ | |
| 413 | ╱ | | | | | 3609 | I | |
| 413 | | | ╱ | | | 3753 | L | |
| 666 | ♥ | | | | | 3776 | ✕ | |
| 703 | ⬆ | | | | | 3846 | ✚ | |

**28w x 32h –** Design stitched on 14 count white Aida using
3 strands for cross stitch, 1 strand for backstitching,
1 strand for French knots.
✎ Cutting line for Aida

# Eleven Pipers Piping

| DMC | X | 1/4 | BS | FK |
|-----|---|-----|----|----|
| white | ☐ | ☐ | | |
| 310 | ■ | ▪ | | |
| 310 | | | ╱ | |
| 413 | | | ╱ | |
| 666 | ♥ | ♥ | | |
| 703 | H | H | | |
| 743 | L | L | | |
| 743 | | | | ● |
| 798 | ◆ | ◆ | | |
| 815 | ╱ | ╱ | | |
| 910 | ⬆ | | | |
| 910 | | | ╱ | |
| 966 | T | T | | |
| 975 | | | ╱ | ● |
| 3774 | ✚ | ✚ | | |

**18w x 36h –** Design stitched on 14 count white Aida using 3 strands for
cross stitch, 1 strand for backstitching, 1 strand for French knots.
✎ Cutting line for Aida

# Puppy on Package

| DMC | X | 1/4 | BS | FK |
|---|---|---|---|---|
| white | ▫ | ▫ | | |
| 402 | T | T | | |
| 413 | | | ╱ | |
| 666 | ♥ | ♥ | | |
| 702 | △ | △ | | |
| 704 | I | I | | |
| 816 | ◢ | ◤ | | |
| 947 | ◣ | ◥ | | |
| 986 | ◆ | ◆ | | |
| 3371 | | ■ | | |
| 3371 | | | ╱ | ● |
| 3776 | ✚ | ✚ | | |
| 3856 | L | L | | |

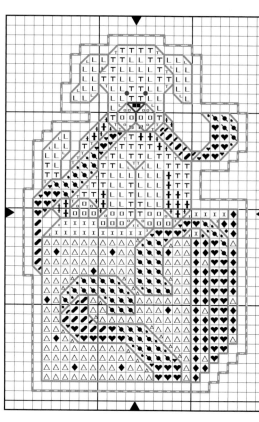

**24w x 37h –** Design stitched on 14 count white Aida using 3 strands for cross stitch, 1 strand for backstitching, 1 strand for French knots.

╱ Cutting line for Aida

# Partridge in a Pear Tree

| DMC | X | 1/4 | BS |
|---|---|---|---|
| white | ▫ | ▫ | |
| 310 | ■ | ■ | |
| 310 | | | ╱ |
| 317 | | | ╱ |
| 355 | | | ╱ |
| 666 | ♥ | | |
| 703 | ▲ | ▲ | |
| 744 | ✚ | ✚ | |
| 762 | L | L | |
| 772 | I | I | |
| 798 | ◆ | | |
| 809 | H | | |
| 910 | | | ╱ |
| 970 | ✚ | ✚ | |
| 975 | ✖ | | |
| 976 | ◣ | ◥ | |
| 3827 | T | T | |

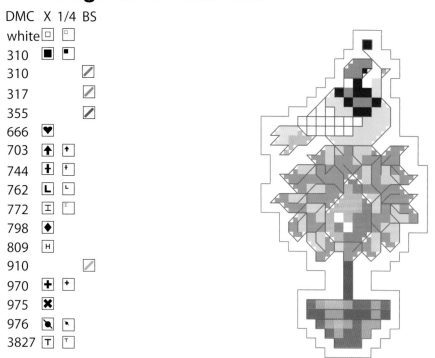

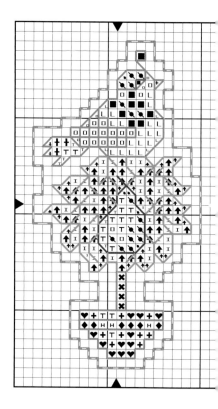

**18w x 34h –** Design stitched on 14 count white Aida using 3 strands for cross stitch, 1 strand for backstitching.

╱ Cutting line for Aida

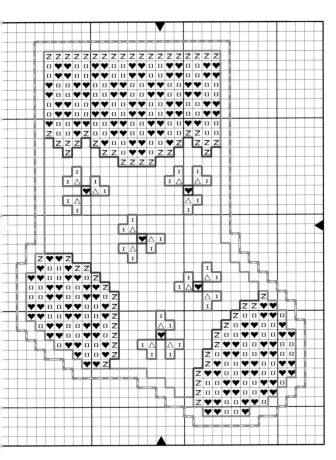

# Checked Stocking

| DMC | X | BS |
|---|---|---|
| white | ▢ | |
| 413 | | ╱ |
| 498 | | ╱ |
| 666 | ♥ | |
| 699 | | ╱ |
| 702 | △ | |
| 704 | I | |
| 956 | Z | |

**31w x 40h** – Design stitched on 14 count white Aida using 3 strands for cross stitch, 1 strand for backstitching.

✎ Cutting line for Aida

# Reindeer Stocking

| DMC | X | 1/4 | BS | FK | | DMC | X | 1/4 | BS | FK |
|---|---|---|---|---|---|---|---|---|---|---|
| white | ▢ | ⊡ | | | | 666 | | | ╱ | ● |
| 310 | | | ╱ | | | 702 | ◤ | | | |
| 310 | | | ╱ | ● | | 702 | | | | ● |
| white | | | ╱ | | | 798 | H | | | |
| 414 | ■ | ◼ | | | | 956 | I | ⊏ | | |
| 415 | ✚ | | | | | 3863 | ◢ | ◿ | | |
| 666 | ♥ | | | | | 3864 | △ | ◸ | | |

**31w x 40h** – Design stitched on 14 count white Aida using 3 strands for cross stitch, 1 strand for backstitching, 1 strand for French knots.

✎ Cutting line for Aida

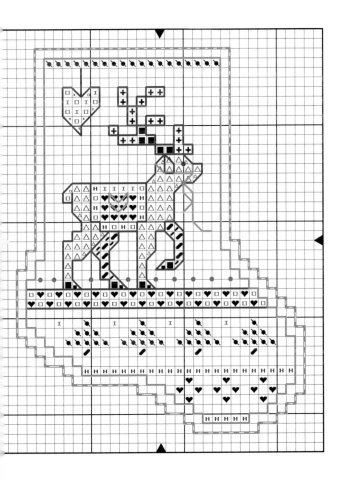

# Santa Head #1

| DMC | X | 1/4 | BS | FK |
|-----|---|-----|-----|-----|
| white | ▢ | ▢ | | |
| 351 | Z | Z | | |
| 647 | ▲ | | | |
| 666 | ♥ | | | |
| 676 | T | | | |
| 729 | ◆ | | | |
| 758 | △ | △ | | |
| 780 | ⬆ | | | |
| 828 | H | | | |
| 844 | ■ | | | |
| 844 | | | ◢ | |
| 898 | | | | ● |
| 911 | ✚ | | | |
| 911 | | | ◢ | |
| 945 | ○ | | | |
| 3072 | L | L | | |

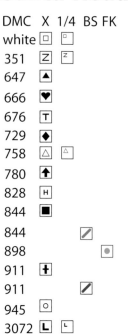

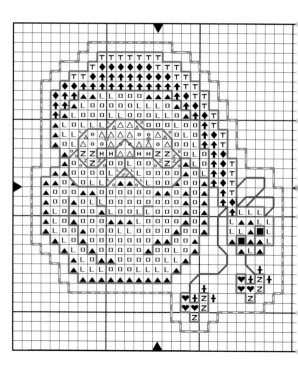

**27w x 30h –** Design stitched on 14 count white Aida using 3 strands for cross stitch, 1 strand for backstitching, 1 strand for French knots.

✂ Cutting line for Aida

# Santa & Cookie

| DMC | X | 1/4 | BS | FK |
|-----|---|-----|-----|-----|
| white | ▢ | ▢ | | |
| 310 | ■ | ■ | | |
| 310 | | | ◢ | |
| 666 | ♥ | ♥ | | |
| 666 | | | | ● |
| 702 | V | V | | |
| 741 | ✚ | | | |
| 775 | L | L | | |
| 815 | ◢ | ◢ | | |
| 890 | ◆ | ◆ | | |
| 910 | ✚ | ✚ | | |
| 910 | | | | ● |
| 956 | ◣ | ◤ | | |
| 963 | H | H | | |
| 3799 | | | ◢ | ● |
| 3826 | ⬆ | ⬆ | | |

**26w x 39h –** Design stitched on 14 count white Aida using 3 strands for cross stitch, 1 strand for backstitching, 1 strand for French knots.

✂ Cutting line for Aida

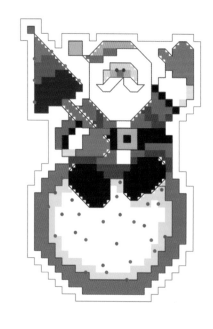
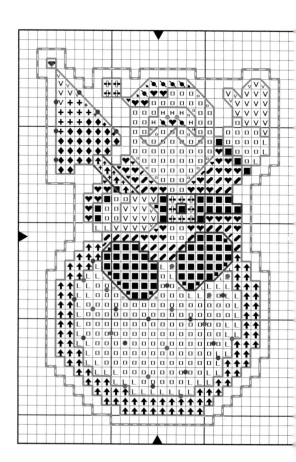

# Roly Poly Santa

| DMC | X | 1/4 | BS | FK |
|---|---|---|---|---|
| white | ☐ | | ☐ | |
| 304 | ◲ | | | |
| 310 | ■ | | | |
| 351 | ◓ | ◓ | | |
| 647 | Z | | | |
| 666 | ♥ | | | |
| 676 | H | | | |
| 677 | I | | | |
| 729 | ▲ | | | |
| 758 | ✚ | + | | |
| 798 | ◆ | | | |
| 799 | ◣ | | | |
| 800 | L | | | |
| 844 | ⬆ | | | |
| 844 | | | ◢ | |
| 898 | | | ◢ | ● |
| 945 | △ | △ | | |
| 3072 | T | | | |

24w x 30h – Design stitched on 14 count white Aida using 3 strands for cross stitch, 1 strand for backstitching, 1 strand for French knots.

◢ Cutting line for Aida

20w x 44h – Design stitched on 14 count white Aida using 3 strands for cross stitch, 1 strand for backstitching, 1 strand for French knots.

◢ Cutting line for Aida

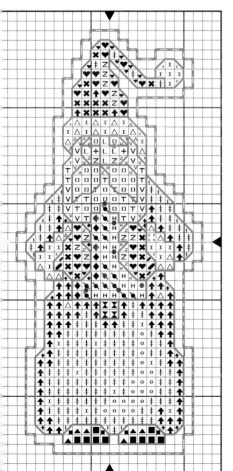

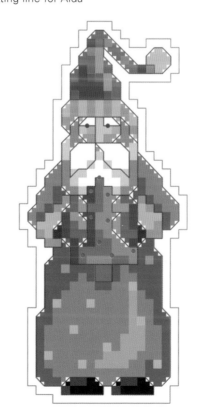

# Folk Art Santa

| DMC | X | 1/4 | BS | FK |
|---|---|---|---|---|
| white | ☐ | ☐ | | |
| 304 | ✖ | | | |
| 310 | ■ | ■ | | |
| 351 | Z | z | | |
| 519 | ◯ | | | |
| 647 | V | V | | |
| 666 | ♥ | ♥ | | |
| 666 | | | | ● |
| 676 | I | I | | |
| 703 | H | H | | |
| 729 | △ | △ | | |
| 758 | ✚ | + | | |
| 798 | ⬆ | ⬆ | | |
| 799 | ‡ | ‡ | | |
| 844 | ▲ | | | |
| 844 | | | ◢ | ● |
| 902 | ◲ | ◢ | | |
| 911 | ◣ | | | |
| 991 | ◆ | ◆ | | |
| 945 | L | | | |
| 3072 | T | T | | |
| 3772 | ✖ | | | |

# Santa Head #2

| DMC | X | 1/4 | BS | FK |
|-----|---|-----|-----|-----|
| white | ▣ | ▢ | | |
| 310 | | | ◪ | ● |
| 413 | | | ◪ | |
| 608 | ⊞ | | | |
| 666 | ♥ | ♥ | | |
| 728 | ✖ | | | |
| 950 | Ｌ | Ｌ | | |
| 956 | Ｈ | | | |
| 3753 | ■ | ■ | | |

**16w x 32h** – Design stitched on 14 count white Aida using 3 strands for cross stitch, 1 strand for backstitching, 1 strand for French knots.

✐ Cutting line for Aida

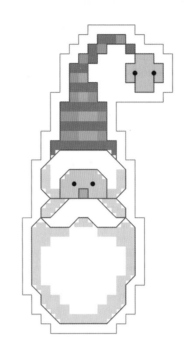

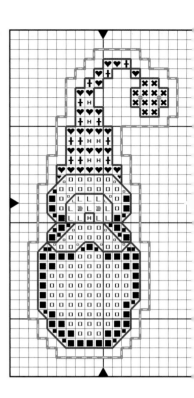

# Snow Reindeer

| DMC | X | BS | FK |
|-----|---|-----|-----|
| white | ▢ | | |
| 304 | ⬆ | | |
| 310 | ■ | | |
| 310 | | ◪ | ● |
| 605 | Ｈ | | |
| 666 | ♥ | | |
| 775 | Ｌ | | |
| 797 | ▲ | | |
| 911 | ✚ | | |
| 913 | Ｚ | | |
| 922 | ✖ | | |
| 977 | ◇ | | |

**32w x 46h** – Design stitched on 14 count white Aida using 3 strands for cross stitch, 1 strand for backstitching, 1 strand for French knots.

✐ Cutting line for Aida

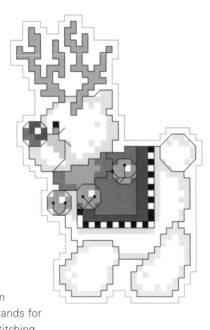

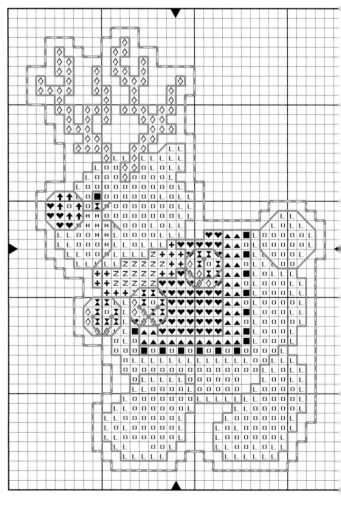

# Santa & Feather Tree

| DMC | X | 1/4 | BS | FK |
|-----|---|-----|-----|-----|
| white | ▫ | | | |
| 310 | ■ | ■ | | |
| 310 | | | ∕ | ● |
| 413 | ▲ | ▲ | | |
| 413 | | | ∕ | |
| 498 | ∕ | ∕ | | |
| 553 | Z | | | |
| 666 | ♥ | ♥ | | |

| DMC | X | 1/4 | BS |
|-----|---|-----|-----|
| 703 | ✚ | | |
| 728 | ◩ | ◣ | ∕ |
| 728 | | | ∕ | |
| 754 | I | | |
| 798 | ◆ | ◆ | |
| 956 | T | | |
| 970 | ✕ | | |
| 3753 | ○ | | |

**32w x 37h –** Design stitched on 14 count white Aida using 3 strands for cross stitch, 1 strand for backstitching, 1 strand for French knots.

∕ Cutting line for Aida

# Santa Head #3

| DMC | X | 1/4 | BS |
|-----|---|-----|-----|
| white | ▫ | ▫ | |
| 304 | ∕ | | |
| 351 | ✚ | | |
| 647 | Z | Z | |
| 666 | ♥ | ♥ | |
| 676 | ⊞ | | |
| 677 | L | L | |
| 703 | ⬟ | | |
| 703 | | | ∕ |

| DMC | X | 1/4 | BS |
|-----|---|-----|-----|
| 729 | ▲ | ▲ | |
| 758 | ○ | ○ | |
| 844 | | | ∕ |
| 898 | ■ | | |
| 898 | | | ∕ |
| 902 | | | ∕ |
| 945 | T | T | |
| 3072 | △ | △ | |

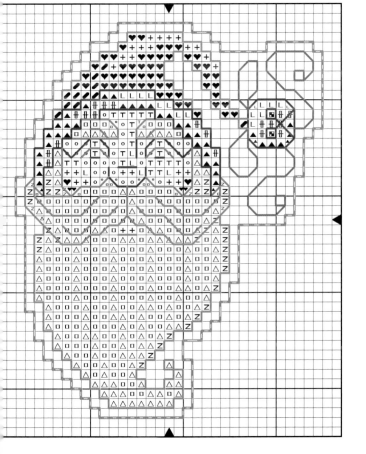

**33w x 41h –** Design stitched on 14 count white Aida using 3 strands for cross stitch, 1 strand for backstitching.

∕ Cutting line for Aida

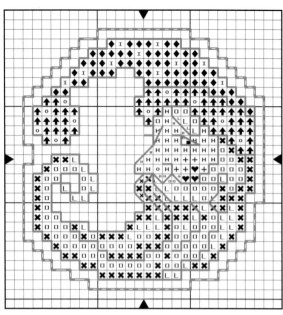

| DMC | X | 1/4 | | DMC | X | 1/4 | BS |
|-----|---|-----|--|-----|---|-----|----|
| white | □ | ▫ | | 729 | ⬆ | | |
| 351 | ➕ | ﹢ | | 798 | ◆ | | |
| 647 | ✖ | ✗ | | 758 | H | H | |
| 666 | ♥ | | | 844 | | ■ | |
| 676 | I | | | 844 | | | ⟋ |
| 677 | ○ | | | 3072 | L | L | |

**26w x 27h** – Design stitched on 14 count white Aida using 3 strands for cross stitch, 1 strand for backstitching.

✎ Cutting line for Aida

# Santa & Bag

| DMC | X | 1/4 | BS | FK | | DMC | X | 1/4 | BS |
|-----|---|-----|----|----|--|-----|---|-----|----|
| white | □ | ▫ | | | | 754 | L | | |
| 310 | ■ | ▪ | | | | 809 | ➕ | | |
| 310 | | | | ● | | 815 | ⟋ | | ⟋ |
| 402 | Z | ᶻ | | | | 956 | T | | |
| 413 | | | ⟋ | | | 3347 | ◆ | | ◆ |
| 553 | H | | | | | 3753 | V | | |
| 666 | ♥ | | | | | 3776 | ✖ | | |

**34w x 38h** – Design stitched on 14 count white Aida using 3 strands for cross stitch, 1 strand for backstitching, 1 strand for French knots.

✎ Cutting line for Aida

# Santa with Penguin

| DMC | X | 1/4 | BS | FK |
|-----|---|-----|-----|-----|
| white | ▣ | ▣ | | |
| 10 | ■ | ■ | ╱ | ● |
| 13 | | | ╱ | |
| 98 | ╱ | | | |
| 66 | ♥ | ♥ | | |
| 03 | H | | | |
| 41 | ▲ | ▣ | | |
| 54 | ✚ | | | |
| 98 | ⊠ | ⊠ | | |
| 09 | L | L | | |
| 10 | ◆ | | | |
| 753 | I | | | |

**34w x 40h** – Design stitched on 14 count white Aida using 3 strands for cross stitch, 1 strand for backstitching, 1 strand for French knots.

✎ Cutting line for Aida

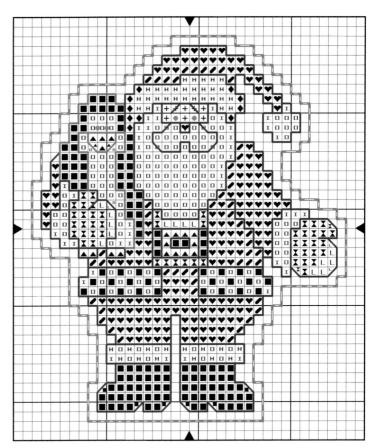

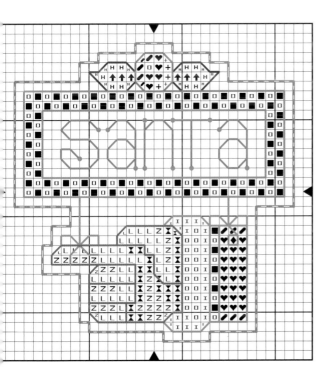

# Santa Sign

| DMC | X | 1/4 | BS | FK |
|-----|---|-----|-----|-----|
| white | ▣ | | | |
| 310 | ■ | | | |
| 310 | | | ╱ | |
| 453 | I | I | | |
| 606 | ✚ | + | | |
| 666 | ♥ | | | |
| 703 | ↑ | | | |
| 742 | ◆ | | | |
| 815 | ╱ | ╱ | | |
| 815 | | | ╱ | ● |
| 910 | | | ╱ | |
| 950 | L | L | | |
| 966 | H | H | | |
| 975 | | | ╱ | |
| 3771 | Z | z | | |
| 3778 | ⊠ | I | | |

**30w x 31h** – Design stitched on 14 count white Aida using 3 strands for cross stitch, 1 strand for backstitching, 1 strand for French knots.

✎ Cutting line for Aida

# Angel with Horn

| X | DMC | 1/4X | B'ST |
|---|---|---|---|
| • | white | ◿ | |
| ◆ | 210 | | |
| ★ | 369 | | |
| ✛ | 402 | | |
| | 414 | | ◿ |
| ▲ | 471 | | |
| ✳ | 712 | | |
| ✔ | 744 | ☐ | |
| ◺ | 758 | | |
| ⦁ | 775 | | |
| | 780 | | ◿ |
| ☐ | 783 | | |
| ♥ | 813 | | |
| > | 818 | ◹ | |
| | 825 | | ◿ * |
| ⊙ | 945 | ☐ | |
| ✕ | 3072 | ☐ | |
| ◉ | 3326 | | |
| ▨ | 3776 | | ◿ |

*Use **2** strands of floss

**40w x 42h** – Design stitched on 14 count ivory Aida using 3 strands for cross stitch, 1 strand for backstitching except where noted.

# Shepherd

| X | DMC | 1/4X | B'ST |
|---|---|---|---|
| • | white | ◿ | |
| ◆ | 210 | | |
| ★ | 369 | ◹ | |
| ✛ | 402 | ◹ | |
| ▼ | 414 | ◹ | ◿ |
| ✕ | 415 | ◹ | |
| ▲ | 471 | | |
| ✔ | 744 | ◹ | |
| ◺ | 758 | ◹ | |
| ⦁ | 775 | ◹ | |
| | 780 | | ◿ |
| ☐ | 783 | | |
| ♥ | 813 | | |
| > | 818 | ◹ | |
| | 825 | | ◿ * |
| ✚ | 841 | | |
| ⊙ | 945 | ☐ | |
| ☆ | 964 | | |
| ◉ | 3756 | ◹ | |
| ▤ | 3776 | ◹ | ◿ |

*Use **2** strands of floss

**40w x 42h** – Design stitched on 14 count ivory Aida using 3 strands for cross stitch, 1 strand for backstitching except where noted.

# Great Joy

| X | DMC | B'ST |
|---|-----|------|
| ◆ | 210 | |
| | 414 | ◿ |
| ✔ | 744 | |
| ⊡ | 775 | |
| ☐ | 783 | |
| ♥ | 813 | |
| ★ | 825 | ◿* |
| ✛ | 3609 | |
| | 3776 | ◿ |
| ◉ | 825 | French Knot |
| ◎ | 3776 | French Knot |

*Use **2** strands of floss

**40w x 42h** – Design stitched on 14 count ivory Aida 3 strands for cross stitch, 1 strand for backstitching except where noted.

# Cherub

| X | DMC | ¼X | B'ST |
|---|-----|-----|------|
| ⊡ | white | ◿ | |
| ◆ | 210 | | |
| ✛ | 402 | | |
| | 414 | | ◿ |
| ⊠ | 415 | | ◸ |
| ◺ | 758 | | ◸ |
| ⊡ | 775 | | |
| | 780 | | ◿ |
| ☐ | 783 | | ◿ |
| ♥ | 813 | | |
| ⊳ | 818 | | |
| | 825 | | ◿* |
| ◯ | 945 | | ☐ |
| ◉ | 3326 | | ◸ |
| ⊟ | 3776 | | ◿ |

* Use **2** strands of floss

**40w x 42h** – Design stitched on 14 count ivory Aida using 3 strands for cross stitch, 1 strand for backstitching except where noted.

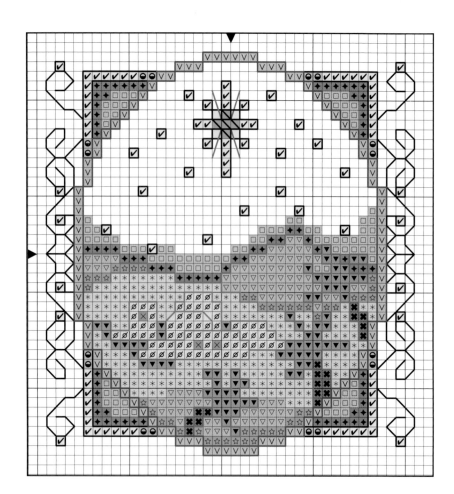

## Town

| X | DMC | 1/4X | B'ST |
|---|-----|------|------|
| V | 210 | | |
| * | 369 | ◺ | |
| ☆ | 402 | | ◹ |
| ▼ | 471 | | |
| ø | 712 | ◺ | |
| ▽ | 738 | | |
| ✔ | 744 | | |
| ☐ | 775 | | |
| ✕ | 780 | | ◹ |
| ◉ | 783 | | |
| ✦ | 813 | | |
| | 825 | | ◹* |
| ✖ | 841 | | |
| | 3776 | | ◹ |

*Use **2** strands of floss.

**40w x 42h** – Design stitched on 14 count ivory Aida using 3 strands for cross stitch, 1 strand for backstitching except where noted.

# Madonna and Child

| X | DMC | 1/4X | B'ST |
|---|-----|------|------|
| • | white | ◹ | |
| V | 210 | | |
| ☆ | 402 | ◺ | |
| | 414 | | ◹ |
| ✔ | 744 | ◺ | |
| ◣ | 758 | ◺ | |
| ☐ | 775 | | |
| | 780 | | ◹ |
| ◉ | 783 | | ◹ |
| ✦ | 813 | | |
| | 825 | | ◹* |
| = | 945 | ◺ | |
| 2 | 959 | ◺ | |
| ◈ | 964 | ◺ | |
| 4 | 3042 | ◪ | |
| ◇ | 3609 | ◺ | |
| ♥ | 3743 | | |
| O | 3756 | ◺ | |
| 5 | 3776 | ◺ | ◹ |

*Use **2** strands of floss

**40w x 42h** – Design stitched on 14 count ivory Aida using 3 strands for cross stitch, 1 strand for backstitching except where noted.

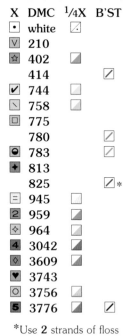

## Wiseman #1

| X | DMC | 1/4X | B'ST |
|---|---|---|---|
| ◆ | 210 | | |
| + | 369 | | |
| | 414 | | / |
| ◒ | 471 | | |
| ☆ | 744 | | / |
| □ | 775 | | |
| | 780 | | / |
| > | 783 | ◩ | / |
| ø | 813 | ◩ | |
| ǁ | 818 | | |
| | 825 | | /* |
| + | 945 | ◩ | |
| 4 | 964 | | |
| ✦ | 3326 | | |
| T | 3609 | | |
| ◎ | 3756 | | |
| ✖ | 3776 | ◩ | / |

*Use **2** strands of floss

**40w x 42h –** Design stitched on 14 count ivory Aida using 3 strands for cross stitch, 1 strand for backstitching except where noted.

## Baby Jesus

| X | DMC | 1/4X | B'ST |
|---|---|---|---|
| • | white | ◩ | |
| ◆ | 210 | | |
| ✧ | 402 | ◩ | |
| ■ | 414 | ◩ | / |
| V | 415 | ◩ | |
| \ | 712 | ◩ | |
| ♡ | 738 | | |
| ☆ | 744 | ◩ | |
| □ | 775 | | |
| ✓ | 780 | ◩ | / |
| > | 783 | ◩ | |
| ø | 813 | | |
| | 825 | | /* |
| ★ | 841 | | |
| + | 945 | ◩ | |
| ✕ | 3072 | ◩ | |
| ✕ | 3743 | | |
| ✖ | 3776 | ◩ | / |

*Use **2** strands of floss

**40w x 42h –** Design stitched on 14 count ivory Aida using 3 strands for cross stitch, 1 strand for backstitching except where noted.

# Manger

| X | DMC | ¼X | B'ST |
|---|---|---|---|
| ⊡ | white | ◹ | |
| ◆ | 210 | | |
| + | 369 | ◹ | |
| | 414 | | ╱ |
| ◙ | 471 | | |
| ▼ | 676 | ◻ | |
| ╲ | 712 | ◻ | |
| ☆ | 744 | | |
| ⊡ | 775 | | |
| ✔ | 780 | | ╱ |
| ▷ | 783 | | ╱ |
| ⊘ | 813 | | |
| ⫴ | 818 | ◻ | |
| | 825 | | ╱* |
| ★ | 841 | | |
| + | 945 | ◻ | |
| ▼ | 959 | ◹ | |
| 4 | 964 | ◹ | |
| ◕ | 3042 | ◹ | |
| ✕ | 3743 | ◹ | |
| ⊙ | 3756 | ◻ | |
| ✖ | 3776 | ◹ | ╱ |

*Use **2** strands of floss

**40w x 42h** – Design stitched on 14 count ivory Aida using 3 strands for cross stitch, 1 strand for backstitching except where noted.

# Wiseman on Camel

| X | DMC | ¼X | B'ST |
|---|---|---|---|
| ⊡ | white | ◹ | |
| ◆ | 210 | ◹ | |
| + | 369 | ◹ | |
| | 414 | | ╱ |
| ▼ | 676 | ◻ | |
| ╲ | 712 | ◻ | |
| = | 738 | ◹ | |
| ☆ | 744 | | |
| ⊡ | 775 | | |
| | 780 | | ╱ |
| ▷ | 783 | | ╱ |
| ⊘ | 813 | ◹ | |
| ⫴ | 818 | | |
| | 825 | | ╱* |
| ★ | 841 | | |
| + | 945 | ◹ | |
| 4 | 964 | ◹ | |
| ◆ | 3326 | | |
| T | 3609 | ◹ | |
| ✕ | 3743 | | |
| ⊙ | 3756 | ◻ | |
| ✖ | 3776 | | ╱ |

*Use **2** strands of floss

**40w x 42h** – Design stitched on 14 count ivory Aida using 3 strands for cross stitch, 1 strand for backstitching except where noted.

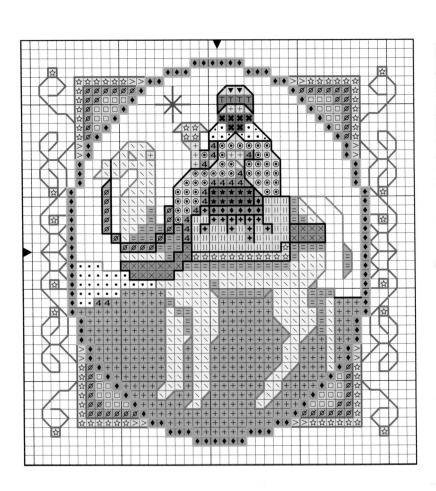

# Wiseman #2

| X | DMC | 1/4X | B'ST |
|---|---|---|---|
| V | 210 | | |
| * | 369 | | |
| | 414 | | ⟋ |
| ▼ | 471 | | |
| ▽ | 738 | | |
| + | 739 | ▨ | |
| ✔ | 744 | | |
| ▢ | 775 | ▨ | |
| | 780 | | ⟋ |
| ◓ | 783 | | ⟋ |
| ✦ | 813 | | |
| ♡ | 818 | ▨ | |
| | 825 | | ⟋* |
| = | 945 | ▨ | |
| 4 | 3042 | ◩ | |
| d | 3326 | ▨ | |
| ◇ | 3609 | | |
| ♥ | 3743 | ◩ | |
| 5 | 3776 | ◩ | ⟋ |
| ★ | 3827 | | |

*Use **2** strands of floss

**40w x 42h** – Design stitched on 14 count ivory Aida using 3 strands for cross stitch, 1 strand for backstitching except where noted.

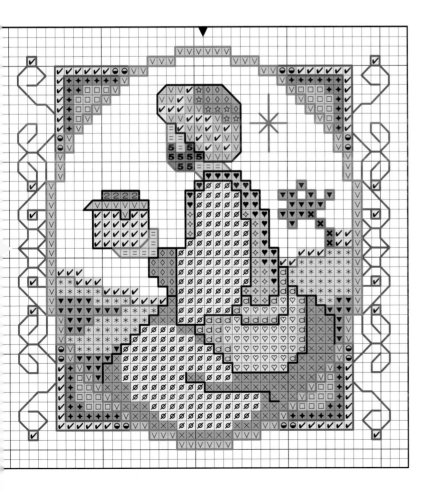

# Wiseman #3

| X | DMC | 1/4X | B'ST |
|---|---|---|---|
| V | 210 | ◩ | |
| * | 369 | | |
| ☆ | 402 | | |
| | 414 | | ⟋ |
| ▼ | 471 | | |
| ✖ | 676 | | |
| ∅ | 712 | | |
| ✔ | 744 | ▨ | |
| ▢ | 775 | | |
| | 780 | | ⟋ |
| ◓ | 783 | | ⟋ |
| ✦ | 813 | | |
| ♡ | 818 | | |
| | 825 | | ⟋* |
| ✖ | 841 | | |
| = | 945 | ▨ | |
| 2 | 959 | | |
| ◇ | 964 | | |
| ♥ | 3072 | | |
| d | 3326 | | |
| ◇ | 3609 | ◩ | |
| 5 | 3776 | ◩ | ⟋ |

*Use **2** strands of floss

**40w x 42h** – Design stitched on 14 count ivory Aida using 3 strands for cross stitch, 1 strand for backstitching except where noted.

# Snowman with Hat

| DMC | X | 1/4 | BS | | DMC | X | 1/4 |
|-----|---|-----|----|----|-----|---|-----|
| white | ▢ | ▢ | | | 703 | Z | |
| 304 | ◢ | | | | 721 | ✕ | ⊠ |
| 310 | ■ | ■ | | | 743 | ▲ | |
| 310 | | | ◢ | | 744 | H | |
| 317 | I | | | | 957 | T | |
| 666 | ♥ | | | | 3756 | L | |
| 700 | ⬆ | | | | | | |

**35w x 48h** – Design stitched on 14 count white Aida using 3 strands for cross stitch, 1 strand for backstitching.

✎ Cutting line for Aida

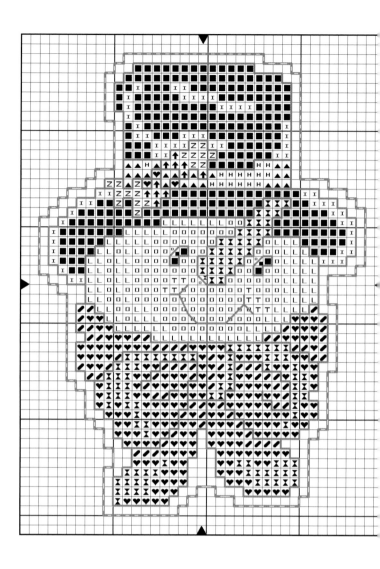

# Snow Bird & Candy Cane

| DMC | X | 1/4 | BS | FK | | DMC | X | 1/4 | BS |
|-----|---|-----|----|----|----|-----|---|-----|----|
| white | ▢ | ▢ | | | | 797 | | | ◢ |
| 310 | | | ◢ | ● | | 911 | ⬆ | | |
| 605 | I | I | | | | 913 | L | | |
| 666 | ♥ | | | | | 971 | ◆ | ◆ | |
| 704 | ◣ | | | | | 977 | H | H | |
| 775 | T | T | | | | | | | |

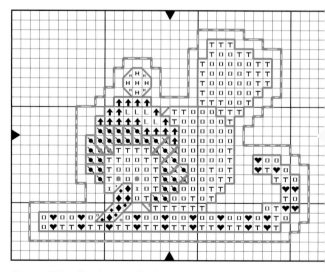

**30w x 22h** – Design stitched on 14 count white Aida using 3 strands for cross stitch, 1 strand for backstitching, 1 strand for French knots.

✎ Cutting line for Aida

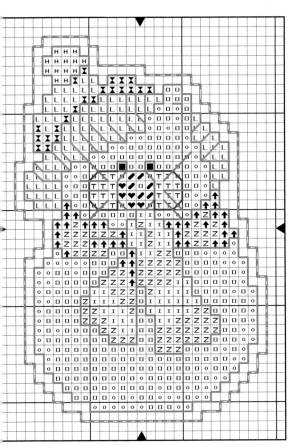

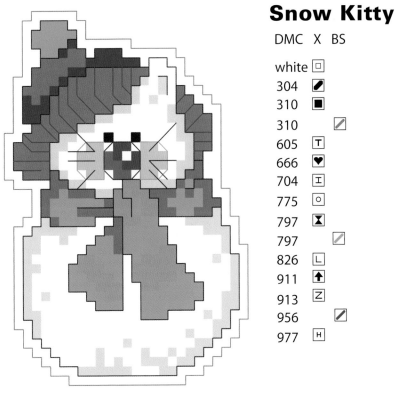

# Snow Kitty

| DMC | X | BS |
|-----|---|----|
| white | ▣ | |
| 304 | ◣ | |
| 310 | ■ | |
| 310 | | ╱ |
| 605 | T | |
| 666 | ♥ | |
| 704 | I | |
| 775 | ○ | |
| 797 | ✕ | |
| 797 | | ╱ |
| 826 | L | |
| 911 | ↑ | |
| 913 | Z | |
| 956 | | ╱ |
| 977 | H | |

**27w x 40h** – Design stitched on 14 count white Aida using 3 strands for cross stitch, 1 strand for backstitching.

▱ Cutting line for Aida

# Starry Snowman

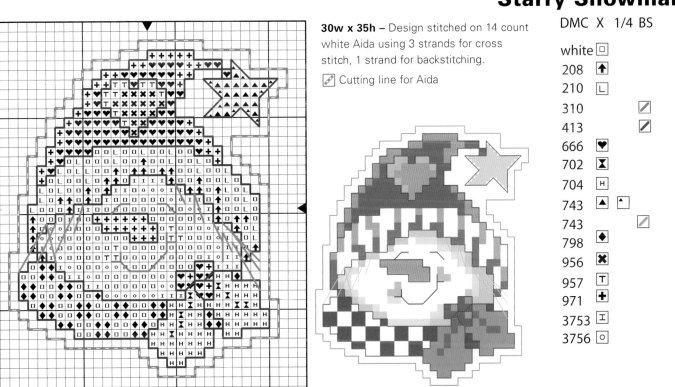

**30w x 35h** – Design stitched on 14 count white Aida using 3 strands for cross stitch, 1 strand for backstitching.

▱ Cutting line for Aida

| DMC | X | 1/4 | BS |
|-----|---|-----|----|
| white | ▣ | | |
| 208 | ↑ | | |
| 210 | L | | |
| 310 | | | ╱ |
| 413 | | | ╱ |
| 666 | ♥ | | |
| 702 | ✕ | | |
| 704 | H | | |
| 743 | ▲ | ◲ | |
| 743 | | | ╱ |
| 798 | ◆ | | |
| 956 | ✕ | | |
| 957 | T | | |
| 971 | ✚ | | |
| 3753 | I | | |
| 3756 | ○ | | |

# Potted Tree

| DMC | X | 1/4 | BS |
|---|---|---|---|
| white | ▫ | | |
| 310 | ■ | | |
| 310 | | | ╱ |
| 666 | ♥ | ♥ | |
| 703 | Z | Z | |
| 742 | ◣ | | |
| 743 | I | | |
| 814 | | | ╱ |
| 815 | ◢ | ◢ | |
| 910 | ✚ | ✚ | |
| 910 | | | ╱ |
| 920 | ✖ | | |
| 902 | | | ╱ |
| 956 | ▲ | ▲ | |
| 970 | H | | |
| 3776 | T | | |
| 3844 | ◆ | | |
| 3846 | ✦ | | |

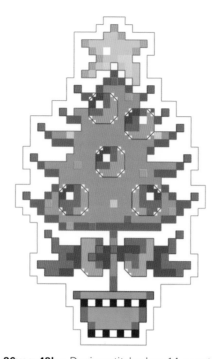

**26w x 43h –** Design stitched on 14 count white Aida using 3 strands for cross stitch, 1 strand for backstitching.

✎ Cutting line for Aida

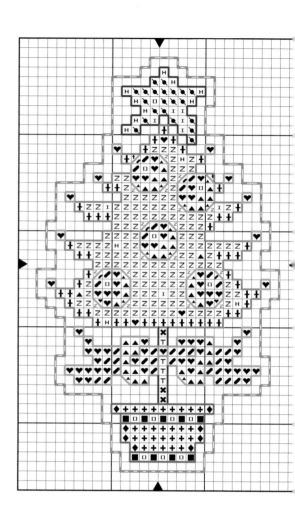

# Patchwork Stocking

| DMC | X | 1/4 | BS | FK |
|---|---|---|---|---|
| white | ▫ | | | |
| 310 | ■ | | | |
| 310 | | | ╱ | ● |
| 453 | ✚ | | | |
| 666 | ♥ | | | |
| 742 | △ | | | |
| 743 | L | L | | |
| 911 | ◆ | | | |
| 956 | 2 | | | |
| 970 | ✚ | ✚ | | |
| 3607 | ✖ | | | |
| 3608 | ◣ | | | |
| 3609 | I | | | |
| 3846 | ⬆ | | | |
| 3846 | | | ╱ | ● |

**28w x 31h –** Design stitched on 14 count white Aida using 3 strands for cross stitch, 1 strand for backstitching, 1 strand for french knots.

✎ Cutting line for Aida

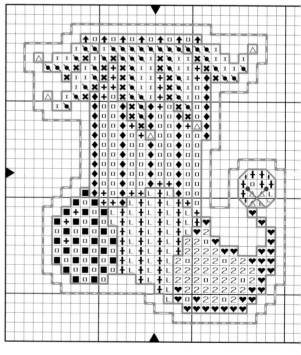

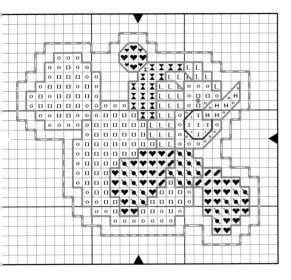

# Snow Bird

| DMC | X | 1/4 | BS | FK | | DMC | X | 1/4 | BS |
|-----|---|-----|----|----|-|-----|---|-----|----|
| white | ☐ | ☐ | | | | 797 | ⊠ | ⊠ | ⁄ |
| 310 | | | ⁄ | ⦿ | | 797 | | | ⁄ |
| 304 | ⁄ | | | | | 826 | L | | |
| 605 | I | I | | | | 956 | ◤ | | |
| 666 | ♥ | ♥ | | | | 956 | | | ⁄ |
| 775 | O | O | | | | 970 | H | H | |

**26w x 22h** – Design stitched on 14 count white Aida using 3 strands for cross stitch, 1 strand for backstitching, 1 strand for French knots.

⁄ Cutting line for Aida

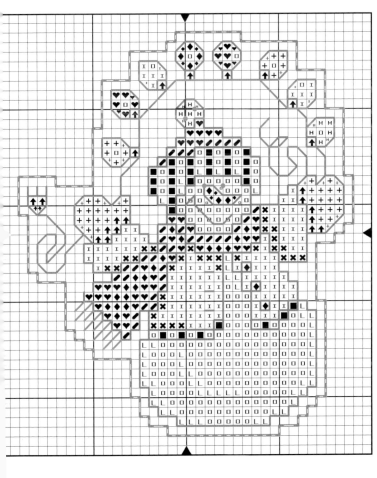

# Snowman with Lights

| DMC | X | 1/4 | BS | FK | | DMC | X | 1/4 | BS |
|-----|---|-----|----|----|-|-----|---|-----|----|
| white | ☐ | ☐ | | | | 700 | ↑ | ↑ | |
| 310 | ■ | | | | | 703 | + | + | |
| 310 | | | ⁄ | ⦿ | | 740 | ◆ | ◆ | |
| 413 | | | ⁄ | | | 742 | H | H | |
| 498 | ⁄ | | | | | 3753 | L | | |
| 666 | ♥ | ♥ | | | | 3844 | ⊠ | | |
| 666 | | | ⁄ | | | 3846 | I | I | |

**36w x 42h** – Design stitched on 14 count white Aida using 3 strands for cross stitch, 1 strand for backstitching, 1 strand for French knots.

⁄ Cutting line for Aida

# Star Cookie

| DMC | X | BS |
|-----|---|-----|
| white | ▫ | |
| 435 | ⬆ | |
| 666 | ♥ | |
| 676 | Z | |
| 703 | ⊠ | |
| 729 | H | |
| 775 | L | |
| 780 | | ✎ |
| 798 | ◆ | |
| 3832 | ◣ | |

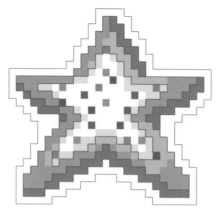

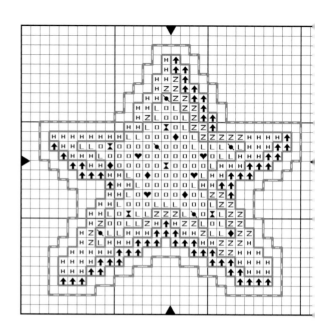

**28w x 26h** – Design stitched on 14 count white Aida using 3 strands for cross stitch, 1 strand for backstitching.

✎ Cutting line for Aida

# Small Stocking & Holly

| DMC | X | 1/4 | BS |
|-----|---|-----|-----|
| white | ▫ | ▫ | |
| 310 | ◼ | ◼ | |
| 413 | | | ✎ |
| 666 | ♥ | ♥ | |
| 702 | ◆ | | |
| 704 | Z | | |
| 956 | L | L | |

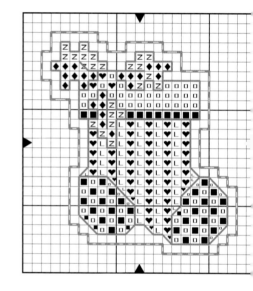

**21w x 23h** – Design stitched on 14 count white Aida using 3 strands for cross stitch, 1 strand for backstitching.

✎ Cutting line for Aida

# Star Santa

| DMC | X | 1/4 | BS |
|-----|---|-----|-----|
| white | ▫ | ▫ | |
| 304 | ▨ | | |
| 310 | ◼ | | |
| 351 | Z | | |
| 519 | ⊡ | | |
| 647 | H | | |
| 666 | ♥ | | |
| 703 | ✚ | | |
| 729 | ◣ | | |
| 758 | ○ | ○ | |
| 798 | ⬒ | | |
| 799 | T | | |
| 844 | | | ✎ |
| 945 | L | | |
| 3072 | △ | | |

**32w x 30h** – Design stitched on 14 count White Aida using 3 strands for cross stitch, 1 strand for backstitching.

✎ Cutting line for Aida

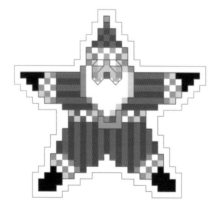

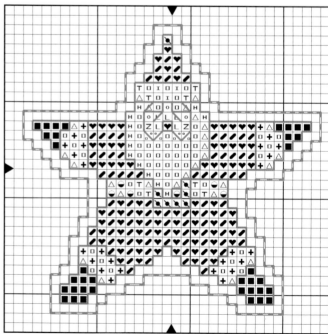

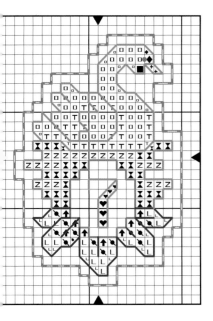

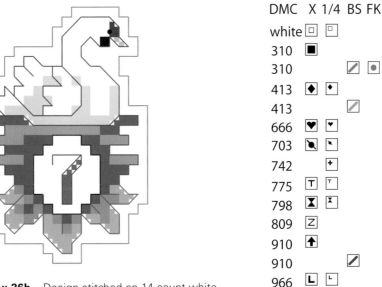

# Seven Swans A-swimming

| DMC | X | 1/4 | BS | FK |
|---|---|---|---|---|
| white | ▢ | ▢ | | |
| 310 | ■ | | | |
| 310 | | | ╱ | ● |
| 413 | ◆ | | ◆ | |
| 413 | | | ╱ | |
| 666 | ♥ | ♥ | | |
| 703 | ◣ | ◥ | | |
| 742 | | | ＋ | |
| 775 | T | T | | |
| 798 | ✕ | ✕ | | |
| 809 | Z | | | |
| 910 | ↟ | | | |
| 910 | | | ╱ | |
| 966 | L | L | | |

**18w x 26h** – Design stitched on 14 count white Aida using 3 strands for cross stitch, 1 strand for backstitching, 1 strand for French knot.
⊘ Cutting line for Aida

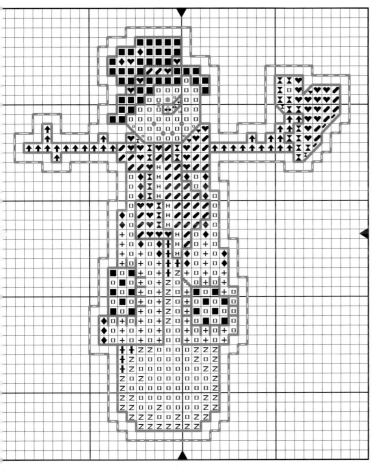

# Tall Snowman

| DMC | X | 1/4 | BS | FK | | DMC | X | 1/4 | BS | FK |
|---|---|---|---|---|---|---|---|---|---|---|
| white | ▢ | ▢ | | | | 816 | ✕ | ✕ | | |
| 310 | ■ | | | | | 910 | ◆ | | | |
| 310 | | | | ● | | 956 | ╱ | ╱ | | |
| 666 | ♥ | ♥ | | | | 963 | H | | | |
| 702 | ＋ | | | | | 3325 | ✚ | | | |
| 741 | ⊞ | ⊞ | | | | 3799 | | | ╱ | ● |
| 775 | Z | | | | | 3826 | ↟ | | | |

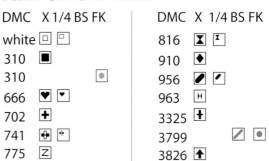

**6w x 43h** – Design stitched on 14 count white Aida using 3 strands for cross titch, 1 strand for backstitching, 1 strand for French knots.
⊘ Cutting line for Aida

# Tall Tree

| DMC | X | 1/4 | BS |
|-----|---|-----|-----|
| 310 | ■ | | |
| 310 | | | ◢ |
| 666 | ♥ | | |
| 702 | ✚ | ✚ | |
| 741 | ◢ | ◢ | |
| 743 | ♠ | ♠ | |
| 744 | H | H | |
| 890 | ◆ | ◆ | |
| 910 | ◪ | ◪ | |
| 956 | ◲ | | |
| 3826 | ⬆ | | |

**14w x 42h –** Design stitched on 14 count white Aida using 3 strands for cross stitch, 1 strand for backstitching.

◢ Cutting line for Aida

# Tree & Ornaments

| DMC | X | BS | | DMC | X | BS |
|-----|---|-----|---|-----|---|-----|
| 100 | ▢ | | | 891 | ✚ | |
| 304 | ◢ | | | 909 | ◆ | |
| 310 | | ◢ | | 909 | | ◢ |
| 333 | ✚ | | | 912 | Z | |
| 340 | ⋈ | | | 975 | H | |
| 349 | ♥ | | | 3854 | ◲ | |
| 720 | ⬆ | | | 3855 | I | |

**36w x 41h –** Design stitched on 14 count white Aida using 3 strands for cross stitch, 1 strand for backstitching.

◢ Cutting line for Aida

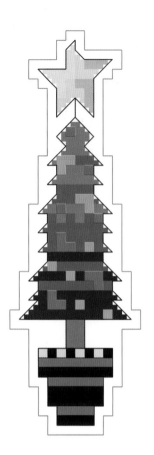

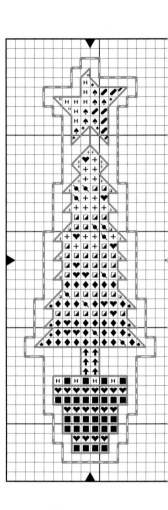

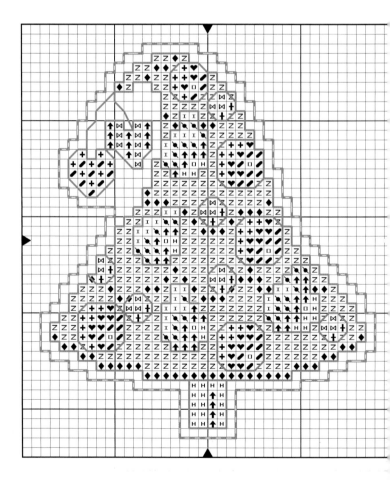

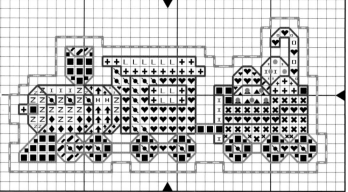

# Train

| DMC | X | 1/4 | BS | FK | | DMC | X | 1/4 | BS | FK |
|-----|---|-----|----|----|----|-----|---|-----|----|----|
| white | □ | ⊡ | | | | 704 | H | | | |
| 310 | ■ | ▪ | | | | 704 | | | | ● |
| 310 | | | ╱ | | | 742 | + | ⊞ | | |
| 334 | Z | ᴢ | | | | 797 | ◆ | ◈ | | |
| 413 | ╱ | ⬦ | | | | 947 | ◣ | | | |
| 413 | | | ╱ | | | 959 | ✕ | ⤬ | | |
| 666 | ♥ | ⧫ | | | | 3607 | ▲ | ▴ | | |
| 666 | | | | ⦿ | | 3846 | I | ⋁ | | |
| 702 | ⬆ | ⬈ | | | | 3855 | L | | | |

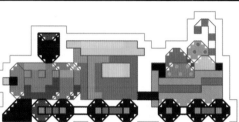

**34w x 16h** – Design stitched on 14 count white Aida using 3 strands for cross stitch, 1 strand for backstitching, 1 strand for French knots.

🖊 Cutting line for Aida

# Two Turtle Doves

| DMC | X | 1/4 | BS | FK | | DMC | X | 1/4 | BS |
|-----|---|-----|----|----|----|-----|---|-----|----|
| white | □ | ⊡ | | | | 703 | Z | ᴢ | |
| 310 | | | ╱ | ⦿ | | 738 | L | ʟ | |
| 317 | ◆ | ◈ | | | | 762 | I | ⋁ | |
| 317 | | | ╱ | | | 904 | ⬆ | ⬈ | |
| 666 | ♥ | ⧫ | | | | 904 | | | ╱ |
| 666 | | | ╱ | ⦿ | | 976 | ╱ | ⬦ | |

**19w x 21h** – Design stitched on 14 count white Aida using 3 strands for cross stitch, 1 strand for backstitching, 1 strand for French knots.

🖊 Cutting line for Aida

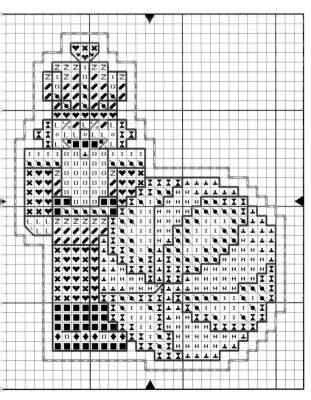

# Nutcracker & Ball

| DMC | X | 1/4 | BS | | DMC | X | 1/4 |
|-----|---|-----|----|----|-----|---|-----|
| white | □ | ⊡ | | | 742 | ◣ | |
| 310 | ■ | ▪ | | | 744 | I | |
| 310 | | | ╱ | | 797 | ╱ | |
| 334 | Z | | | | 947 | ✕ | |
| 413 | ◆ | | | | 951 | L | ʟ |
| 413 | | | ╱ | | 956 | ⊥ | |
| 666 | ♥ | ⧫ | | | 957 | H | ʜ |
| 741 | ✕ | ⋈ | | | 3326 | O | |

**29w x 35h** – Design stitched on 14 count white Aida using 3 strands for cross stitch, 1 strand for backstitching.

🖊 Cutting line for Aida

# GENERAL INSTRUCTIONS

## Working with Charts

Each colored square or square with a symbol on a chart represents one Cross Stitch. Each colored triangle or reduced symbol on a chart represents one Quarter Stitch. Colored dots represent French Knots. The straight lines on a chart indicate Backstitch. When a French Knot or Backstitch covers a square, the symbol may be omitted or reduced and placed on both sides of the Backstitch. When identical symbols are shown on both sides of a Backstitch, a full Cross Stitch is worked and then the Backstitch.

Each chart is accompanied by a color key. This key indicates the color of floss to use for each stitch. The headings on the color key are for Cross Stitch (X), DMC color number (DMC), Quarter Stitch (1/4 or ¼X), Backstitch (B'ST or BS), and French Knot (FK). Color key columns should be read vertically and horizontally to determine type of stitch and floss color.

## Stitch Diagrams

**Cross Stitch:** Work one Cross Stitch to correspond to each square on the chart. For horizontal rows, work stitches in two journeys (**Fig. 1**). For vertical rows, complete each stitch as shown (**Fig. 2**). When the chart shows a Backstitch crossing a colored square (**Fig. 3**), a Cross Stitch should be worked first, then the Backstitch (**Fig. 6**) should be worked on top of the Cross Stitch.

**Fig. 1**

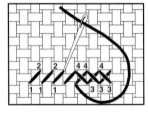

**Fig. 2**

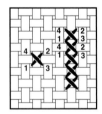

**Fig. 3**

**Half Cross Stitch:** This stitch is one journey of the Cross Stitch and is worked from lower left to upper right as shown in **Fig. 4**.

**Fig. 4**

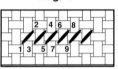

**Quarter Stitch:** Quarter Stitches are denoted by triangular shapes of color or reduced symbols. Come up at 1, then split fabric thread to go down at 2 (**Fig. 5**).

**Fig. 5**

**Backstitch:** For outline detail, Backstitch (shown as colored straight lines) should be worked after the design has been completed (**Fig. 6**).

**Fig. 6**

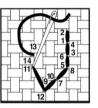

**French Knot:** Bring needle up at 1. Wrap floss once around needle and insert needle at 2, holding end of floss with non-stitching fingers (**Fig. 7**). Tighten knot, then pull needle through fabric, holding floss until it must be released. For larger knot, use more strands; wrap only once.

**Fig. 7**

# TIPS & TECHNIQUES

## WORKING ON PERFORATED PLASTIC

Quarter stitches cannot be used when stitching on perforated plastic. Replace quarter stitches with full cross stitches or simply omit the quarter stitches completely.

## MAKING A PADDED SHAPE

1. For pattern, cut a piece of tracing paper the desired finished size, or trace pattern listed in instructions.
2. Use pattern to cut one piece of cardboard and one piece of batting.
3. Trim stitched piece to 1" larger on all sides than pattern.
4. Glue quilt batting to cardboard. Center cardboard, batting side down, on wrong side of stitched piece. Checking frequently to make sure design stays centered, fold fabric edges over to back of cardboard and glue in place.

## ADDING FABRIC-COVERED CORDING

1. Make cording by cutting a length of 2"w bias cut fabric (length will depend on how many designs you are trimming). Cut a piece of $1/8$" diameter cord the same length. Center cord on wrong side of bias strip. Using a zipper foot and stretching gently as you sew, match long fabric edges and sew as close as possible to cord.
2. Add cording to padded shape by beginning 1" from one end of cord at center bottom of padded shape. Glue cording around padded shape until it almost meets the beginning end. Trim cording end about 2" from beginning. Remove $1\frac{1}{2}$" of stitches from cording end and pull bias strip away from cord. Cut cord ends so they meet exactly. Fold end of loose bias strip $1/2$" to wrong side, and rewrap strip around both ends of cording; glue in place.

## ADDING TWISTED FLOSS CORDING

1. Knot floss ends together to form a loop. Holding the knot in one hand, hook floss over a drawer knob and pull floss tight. Keeping floss pulled tight, twist floss clockwise until it begins to twist back on itself.
2. Hold floss at midpoint with free hand, then fold knotted end to meet end at knob and hold ends together. Let midpoint go to allow floss to twist. Knot floss ends together at knob and cut twisted cord from knob. Pull twisted cord between fingers to smooth.
3. Glue cording to ornament as shown in **Fig. 1**.

**Fig. 1**

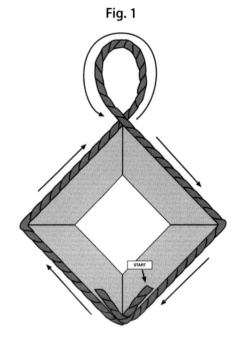

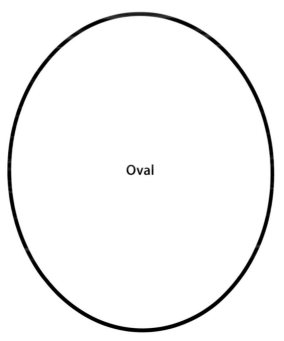

Oval

# FINISHING INSTRUCTIONS

Here's how we stitched and finished the ornaments. Mix and match the instructions to create a custom ornament that fits perfectly into your seasonal decor!

The ornaments (front cover) are stitched on 14 count white Aida. Use 3 strands of floss for Cross Stitch and 1 strand for all other stitches unless noted.

Glue stitched piece to felt. When completely dry, trim fabric and felt to 1 square from design.

The small ornaments and mini stockings (pages 2, 6 and 7) are stitched on 14 count white perforated plastic. Use 3 strands of floss for Cross Stitch and 1 strand for all other stitches unless noted.

Glue stitched piece to white paper. Trim plastic and paper to 1 square from design.

For the mini stockings, glue design to colored cardstock. Use decorative-edge scissors to trim excess cardstock.

Santa's workshop ornaments (page 1) are stitched on 14 count white Aida. Use 3 strands of floss for Cross Stitch and 1 strand for all other stitches unless noted.

Using 2 floss strands, work a running stitch about $1/2$" from edges of design.

Fuse lightweight interfacing and paper-backed fusible web to wrong side of Aida. Trim Aida to $1/4$" from running stitches.

For backing, cut 2 fabric pieces slightly larger than trimmed design. Use fusible web to fuse fabric pieces wrong sides together.

Fuse trimmed design to center of backing. Use pinking shears to trim backing.

The penguin ornaments (page 4) are stitched on 14 count white Aida. Use 3 strands of floss for Cross Stitch and 1 strand for all other stitches unless noted.

Make design into a padded shape, using a square pattern cut the same size as the stitched area.

Glue a fabric or felt backing to padded shape. Glue padded shape to a purchased 6"w plastic snowflake ornament.

The oval ornaments (page 3) are stitched on 14 count Ivory Aida. Use 3 strands of floss for Cross Stitch and 1 strand for all other stitches unless noted.

Make design into a padded shape, using the oval pattern on page 63.

Add twisted floss cording, using a 72" floss length. Glue a fabric backing to padded shape.

The Santa square ornaments (page 3) are stitched on 14 count white Aida. Use 3 strands of floss for Cross Stitch and 1 strand for all other stitches unless noted.

Make design into a padded shape, using a square pattern about $1/4$" larger than the stitched area.

Add fabric-covered cording. Glue a fabric or felt backing to padded shape.

Santa's bake shop ornaments (page 4) are stitched on 14 count Ivory Aida. Use 3 strands of floss for Cross Stitch and 1 strand for all other stitches unless noted.

Fuse lightweight interfacing and paper-backed fusible web to wrong side of Aida. Trim Aida to $1/2$" from design.

For backing, cut 2 fabric pieces slightly larger than trimmed design. Use fusible web to fuse fabric pieces wrong sides together.

Fuse trimmed design to center of backing. Use pinking shears to trim backing.

For hanging loops, trim ends of two $3 1/2$" lengths of $3/8$"w grosgrain ribbon into points. Glue ends to front and back of ornament.

The Nativity ornaments (page 5) are stitched on 14 count Ivory Aida. Use 3 strands of floss for Cross Stitch and 1 strand for all other stitches unless noted.

Make design into a padded shape, using a square pattern about $1/4$" larger than the stitched area.

Beginning 1" from end, glue purchased metallic cording around edges of padded shape. Glue cording ends to back of padded shape.

For hanger, fold a 6" length of metallic cording in half; glue ends to back of ornament. Slide a bead over hanger; glue to secure.

Glue a fabric backing to padded shape.

Library of Congress Control Number: 2019933134

Made in USA.

We have made every effort to ensure that these instructions are accurate and complete. We cannot, however, be responsible for human error, typographical mistakes, or variations in individual work.